Bagels and Grits

This book was published with the generous support
of the George L. Mosse/Laurence A. Weinstein Center
for Jewish Studies at the University of Wisconsin–Madison.

In memory of
LAURENCE A. WEINSTEIN

Bagels and Grits

A Jew on the Bayou

Jennifer Anne Moses

Terrace Books
A trade imprint of the University of Wisconsin Press

Terrace Books, a trade imprint of the University of Wisconsin Press, takes its name from the Memorial Union Terrace, located at the University of Wisconsin–Madison. Since its inception in 1907, the Wisconsin Union has provided a venue for students, faculty, staff, and alumni to debate art, music, politics, and the issues of the day. It is a place where theater, music, drama, literature, dance, outdoor activities, and major speakers are made available to the campus and the community.
To learn more about the Union, visit www.union.wisc.edu.

Terrace Books
A trade imprint of the University of Wisconsin Press
1930 Monroe Street, 3rd Floor
Madison, Wisconsin 53711-2059

www.wisc.edu/wisconsinpress/

3 Henrietta Street
London WC2E 8LU, England

5   4   3   2   1

Printed in the United States of America

Library of Congress Cataloging-in-Publication Data
Moses, Jennifer Anne.
Bagels and grits : a Jew on the bayou / Jennifer Anne Moses.
        p.   cm.
        ISBN 0-299-22440-6 (cloth : alk. paper)
1. Moses, Jennifer Anne—Homes and haunts—Louisiana—Baton Rouge.
    2. Moses, Jennifer Anne—Religion. 3. Jewish women—Louisiana—
    Baton Rouge—Biography.   4. Baton Rouge (La.)—Biography.   I. Title.
F379.B33M67   2007
976.3′180049240092—dc22   2007011823
[B]

For this book, some names have been changed to protect the privacy of the individuals described herein. The poem "Birth Is a Beginning" by Rabbi Alvin Fine is reproduced by permission of the Central Conference of American Rabbis. Parts of chapters 1, 6, 8, and 12 appeared in modified form in *Commentary* (reprinted from the March 2002 issue by permission; all rights reserved), *The Washington Post Magazine, The Washington Post Magazine,* and *Notre Dame Magazine,* respectively.

For ABBA

Before his death, Rabbi Zusya said: "In the coming world, they will not ask me: 'Why were you not Moses?' They will ask me: 'Why were you not Zusya?'"

From Martin Buber's *Tales of the Hasidim*

Stanley is driving in Jerusalem. He's late for a meeting. He's looking for a parking space, but he can't find one. In desperation, he turns toward Heaven and says, "God, if you find me a parking space, I promise that I'll eat only kosher, respect *Shabbat,* and observe all the holidays."

Miraculously, a place opens up just in front of him.

He turns his face up to heaven and says, "Never mind, I just found one."

A joke going around the internet during the summer of 2005

Contents

Bagels and Grits

1

With God in Baton Rouge

I'm driving my minivan down Florida Boulevard in Baton Rouge, Louisiana, past the Snack Shack, the Ford dealership, the U-Lock-It, and the Super Chicken, listening to Lorraine, who is sitting in the seat next to me, talking. It's a hot, sticky October day—the overcast sky like a blanket, keeping the heat in. Louisiana weather is like no other I've ever experienced—so hot and so oppressive for so many months that it feels personal, like the entire planet is soon to catch fire and you'd better get off it before it's too late—and for the millionth time since moving here a few years ago from Washington, D.C., I yearn for cooler pastures, for the smell of falling autumn leaves, for crisp apples and cold nights and sweater weather. But I'm here, in Baton Rouge, with Lorraine, and Lorraine likes to talk. Correction: Lorraine loves to talk—and to smoke, sing, eat, anything that will keep her mouth moving. She is forty-four, so dark that her skin shines like polished mahogany, and growing fat from all the potato chips and pork rinds that she eats when she's not talking.

"Honey, let me tell you," she is saying. "How I get here? Don't rightly know. Didn't mean to get here, but here I am. Lord Jesus. Jesus loves me, you know? Loves you, too. He do, even if you don't know it, but he do."

I nod.

"How many children you got?" she says, changing the subject.

"Three," I answer.

"How old are they?"

My eldest, Sam, is twelve, I tell her, and my twins, Rose and Jonathan, are eight. There's a lot more that I could tell her about them—such as the fact that Sam is so physically beautiful that I fear for him; or that Jonathan, at birth, looked like a baby bird, all beaky and bony, with downy fur; or that Rose is so content within her skin that it's as if she'd been born with the soul of a shaman—but I don't. It would be like delivering a discourse on quantum physics to a dying man. So I keep quiet, waiting for the story that I know is coming—the one about how Lorraine landed in prison. She's told it before, but because her mind doesn't work quite right, she doesn't remember.

"Ain't that nice, now," she says in her smoker's contralto. "Two boys and a girl. Praise Jesus. Bet they favor you. My own children, I got two boys and three girls, all grown. First there's Larry, he make me a grand-mother first. His father was something else. Lord, I loved that man. Would have done anything for him, sure enough. I give him three fine children. Three fine ones, and what he do? I was working up at the printing press then. Had me a good job. Steady. I was going to school, too. LSU. Work-ing full shift every day of the week, don't you know it, child, and going to school, too. Come home. What do I see? That man in bed with my favor-ite auntie. My favorite damn auntie. Mamma's youngest sister, don't you know. Caught them in my own damn bed. Didn't think nothing about it. Just ran into the kitchen, grabbed me the gun in the cabinet, and shot that motherfucker right in the head. Missed and shot him again. 'Cause I wanted to kill that mother dead."

She looks out the window, begins to hum along with the radio. "Shot him good," she says. "Spent a week in the hospital. But you know, he still living."

"Do you mind if I turn the radio down?"

"Still out there catting around. But me, I get sent down to St. Gabriel," she says, referring to the Louisiana Correctional Institute for Women. "Five years in St. Gabriel. Got out for good behavior. But five years, five years plenty long, and I ain't lying."

I turn the radio down.

"But you know, it when I get out that the trouble started. While I locked up I good as gold, but when I get out, oh, Lord, that's when things start going bad for real. Stayed with my mamma, and got a job, sure enough. Working at the dry-cleaning plant. But every day I come home, and I do a little stuff. Every damn day. Relieve my pain. One day, though, everything change: I come home, and set everything out, all easy like. I got my cocaine right here on the table, right in front of me, like I always do. I got my beer right next to it, nice and cold, straight from the refrigerator. And my pack of cigarettes. That's when I heard it."

An SUV filled with frat boys tailgates us for a couple of blocks, and then, with a roar, passes on the left going about seventy miles an hour, rock music blaring out the open windows, purple and yellow LSU flags fluttering in the wind.

"That's when you heard what, Lorraine?"

"I reach for the cocaine, but that's when Jesus call me. Heard him as clearly as I hear you. And Jesus said, 'Lorraine, my love, put that down.' So I reached for the beer, and Jesus said, 'Lo, my love, put that down.' He took the taste for it right out of my mouth. So then I reached for the cigarette, but he didn't say anything. Which is how I know I still have his permission to smoke."

This part of the story is new to me.

"I'm truly blessed," Lorraine says, turning up the music once again, running her tongue over her lips.

"Yes indeed," she adds.

Lorraine has AIDS. Her brother, who was a cross-dresser and a prostitute until his own death from AIDS just a few weeks ago, had lost his vision, then his ability to control his bladder, and finally his sense of his own individuality, while Lorraine, frantic, had clucked over him, rolling her eyeballs around in her head, moaning and crying. But Lorraine doesn't seem aware that she, too, could succumb to the more dismal ravages of AIDS—though it's hard to tell what exactly Lorraine does or does not understand, because her brain is slowly being eaten away by disease, *cytomegalovirus ventriculoencephalitis,* to be precise. She forgets things, like whether or not she still needs to go to the bathroom, and what your name is.

"You just got to believe," she says.

Which is a good one, given that, though I admire what appears to be Lorraine's deep-seated faith, and even envy it, I myself am not entirely sure that there is a God at all.

"Just got to call on Jesus," she adds.

And that's another thing: I'm Jewish and, hence, do not make a practice of calling on Jesus, ever. Jesus, for me, is nothing but a burden, a poor sap of a Jewish boy appearing out of the tragic, bloody history of Roman Palestine, a mystic who was used, abused, and finally tortured to death, so that later followers of his could claim his divinity and start killing other people on account of it. Not that I'm inclined to discuss my religious identity with Lorraine, not to mention the peculiar responsibility of being among the dwindling remnant of what was, before the Second World War, a large and vibrant people, with its own culture, language, and philosophy—the great Ashkenazi civilization that first took root in the Rhineland more than a thousand years ago, conversing and writing in the three Jewish languages of Hebrew, Aramaic, and Yiddish, as well as dozens of European tongues, eventually giving the world the Ba'al Shem Tov (the "Master of the Good Name") on the one hand, and Woody Allen on the other. Nor, I think, would it be a good idea to clue her in. Lorraine's knowing that I'm a Jew would just complicate things, and I don't want to get into a big theological discussion with her about why I haven't accepted Jesus as my personal savior or deliver a capsule history of Christian anti-Semitism, starting with the popes' injunctions to segregate Jews in ghettos, moving up through the Inquisition, and ending with the Holocaust, smack in the heart of Christian Europe, with a postscript concerning the assorted cranks and Bible-thumpers right here in Baton Rouge who aren't exactly what you'd call friendly toward my people, unless you consider converting us en masse in order to bring about the End of Days as predicted in the book of Revelations a friendly gesture. But what does Lorraine or, for that matter, anyone I know, have to do with all of that? Lorraine simply loves Jesus, and she wants me to, too.

Which is no real surprise: you can't live in Baton Rouge without bumping up against Jesus just about every time you walk out of the house, not only on your doorstep in the form of local missionaries but also on your neighbors' lips, on the towering crosses that dot the highways, on bus stop benches that proclaim JESUS IS THE ANSWER, on the airwaves, in the letters-to-the-editor column of the local newspaper, and especially in the hundreds of churches that seem to define—even more than petrochemical plants and shotgun houses and Spanish moss–draped live oak trees—this particular corner of the world.

Ephesus Apostolic; Hosanna First Assembly; Antioch Full Gospel Baptist; Remnant of God; Church of God in Christ; Destiny International; Highway to Glory Worship Center; I've Had Enough Outreach Ministries; House of Judah; Holy Trinity; Holy Saints; Holy Mary Mother of God; St. Alban's; St. Luke's; St. James; True Believers Christian Congregation; Abundant Everlasting Life Fellowship. The Sunshine Pages has eleven full pages of listings, three columns each. There are more churches than there are schools, more churches than there are restaurants, and certainly more churches than there are synagogues.

"Take your pain to Jesus, honey," Lorraine says, as much to herself as to me. And then, looking straight at me, she says, "You a good Christian, child. You really is."

Lorraine lives, along with eleven other HIV-positive adults, at St. Anthony's, a residential treatment facility where I began doing volunteer work one morning a week shortly after my twins started kindergarten. I signed on for this job chiefly because I wanted to give something back to a community that, for no discernible reason, had put me and my family on easy street, and also because Jewish tradition, along with rules about honoring one's parents, burying the dead, and rejoicing with bride and bridegroom, instructs us to visit the sick. The Talmud goes so far as to say that he who doesn't perform this commandment is like one who sheds blood, the Gemara relating the words of Rabbi Aha bar Hanina, that anyone who visits the sick takes away one sixtieth of his or her pain. Not that I was steeped in rabbinic lore: I just thought that it was time already for me to do something other than sit in my kitchen, reading the newspaper and eating my own liver out over global warming. Plus my twins—thank God—were finally in school full-time, in Big Kid school where they ate hot lunches on little chairs in the cafeteria and came home smelling like chalk dust and canned green beans, meaning that I would have my days back again, that I could take a nap and go to the bathroom without being followed. In short, for the first time since Sam was born in 1989, when I was thirty, I had enough time to myself.

I had another reason for choosing this particular kind of work: my mother, more than a thousand miles away in the same house in Virginia where I grew up, had been struggling with ovarian cancer for years, and from such a distance there was next to nothing I could do to comfort her.

Nor did I have any way of understanding what was happening to her, the *why* of it, the sheer pomposity of a disease that had had the chutzpah to turn my athletic, overbearing, energetic, and enormously warm mother into an invalid and along the way upend a family myth that, roughly, dictated that the superiority of the family genes would shield and protect its members from affliction. The idea was that, in my family, we didn't get sick: sickness was for other people—for ordinary people, the kind of sorry-assed raggle-draggle folks you see lugging whining kids around the shopping mall or fighting with their spouses at a family-style restaurant. My mother's cancer was an affront to that; a giant in-your-face *so what?* But if I couldn't help Mom, or understand why she had to suffer, I could at least look into the face of death itself, or into the faces of the dying, and in this way perhaps prepare myself for things to come. Plus, if I were being completely honest, I also wanted to see if I could take it. I wanted to know if I, the ultimate wee-nie, the girl who cried whenever Mary Tyler Moore threw her hat up into the air at the beginning of the *Mary Tyler Moore Show,* had the stuff.

I grew up in a large, white, starkly modern house surrounded by woods and streams in McLean, Virginia, the second of four children of assimi-lated, athletic, well-educated, and wealthy German Jews who traced their families back over the generations to the town of Gross-Rapperhausen, in the state of Hesse, on my father's side, and sixteenth-century Bavaria, on my mother's. In addition to me, my two sisters, one brother, parents, and our housekeeper, a regal and kind black woman named Mae Carter, our household included, at any given time, two or three dogs, any number of guinea pigs, assorted hamsters, a canary named Tweety Bird, turtles, stray frogs, and various au pairs. Annette, from Ireland; Flora, from Scotland; Alfreida, from Trinidad: we went through them like a teenage boy goes through socks. There was also, for a time at least, a horse, Massy (short for Massasoit, the Indian chieftain), whom I rode to glory one July day in 1968 at the Cobbler Mountain Horse and Pony Show, in Delaplane, Virginia. I still have the silver cup I won that afternoon, and occasionally I find myself gazing at it, in complete wonder, as if it were an artifact brought back from another time and place entirely.

The idea to do AIDS work—rather than, say, volunteer in an old-age home or a hospital—came to me after my husband, Stuart, and I saw an excellent production of *Angels in America* at Louisiana State University. After the show, I noticed a pile of pamphlets about AIDS on a table in the lobby, picked one up, and took it home. Some months later, after enduring a morning-long "orientation session" consisting of watching out-of-date videos about condom use, I went to St. Anthony's Home for the first time. Chuck Johnson, the house manager, gave me a tour of the place—laundry room, kitchen, lounge, therapeutic bath—and told me to take it slow, that if I didn't I'd burn out. Then he said, "Why don't you go and introduce yourself to the residents?" I did as I was told, but as I went from room to room, I felt that I'd turned into a cheerleader, or perhaps an airline hostess. *Hi! I'm Jennifer! And I'm going to be volunteering here! Let me know if there's anything I can do to help. Only please don't ask me to handle your bodily fluids, because I don't want to die!* I was positively dripping with bullshit. I was also terrified. But my terror didn't really have anything to do with my irrational fear of AIDS, because in order to contract HIV you have to work hard at it, for example by becoming a prostitute. Intravenous drug use will do it too, as will unprotected sex with any of a variety of HIV-positive partners. Though I'd been a hypochondriac all my life, even I didn't lose sleep over the thought that one day, if I spent enough time among the sick at St. Anthony's, I too might contract HIV. What I lost sleep over was cancer. But I really was scared. Scared that at any moment one of the residents would sniff out my mealy-mouthed, do-gooding pretensions, see right through my perky exterior to my barbed and cramped heart, and expose me. Scared of my incompetence, my lack of center. What was I doing there? I was a struggling writer, a nice Jewish girl with a history of depression from a wealthy East Coast family, the wife of a university professor, a person who obsessed about the contents of the *New York Times Book Review* and spent her summers on a crystal-clear lake in Maine. That first day at St. Anthony's I felt like I was standing on the edge of the abyss, a hair's breadth away from chaos. Everyone looked like an inmate of Auschwitz, only, unlike most Jews, most of the residents of St. Anthony's were black. Chuck told me that volunteers put in an average of six months. That gave me until February, when I'd be able to quit with some semblance of self-respect intact.

That being said, my job at St. Anthony's chiefly involves running errands and reading the New Testament aloud, which at times, given the anti-Jewish passages, is discomfiting. Also, hanging out with the residents—most of whom are destitute, barely educated, and addicted—and taking them to doctors' and dentists' appointments. That's why I'm out now, driving around Baton Rouge on a typically disgustingly hot and humid day. Lorraine had wanted to get cigarettes. Then she wanted to get a six-pack of Coke. Then she wanted to go back to the discount cigarette store and get a lighter.

One problem with the job—I'm thinking as Lorraine and I tool along—is that it's boring. Drive to the KFC for a tub of drumsticks. That's all drumsticks—I don't want no breasts. Go to the one on Tom Drive. Yeah, it open now. Open at ten. Drive to the Winn Dixie for a package of hot sausage. Got to be spicy hot sausage, the kind that come in the four-pack, right? Drive to the Wal-Mart for some underwear and also I want some Halloween candy and also some hand cream. Damn this stuff so expensive, got a dollar you can lend me? Hang out, watching *Little House on the Prairie* reruns. Hang out, watching the mosquitoes swarm on the patio out back. Hang out, talking about Miss Marie's ex-husband, the damn scum, no child, didn't need no more scumbag husband hanging round me, I go get me a divorce.

The other problem is, people die.

Geraldine died in November 1998. She was my first. She was also the first resident who I felt comfortable with. When I started volunteering, she was the only woman among the eleven men living at St. Anthony's and by far the friendliest toward me. At the time, St. Anthony's was filled with strong personalities, most of whom had carved out specific roles for themselves in the life of the little community. There was Tommy, who mainly lay in bed staring off into space, but who, it turned out, had once been a high school math teacher. Now he was gentle and hopeful, proud of his degrees from Southern University, and close to his sister, a social worker who came every morning to visit with him before going off to work. Every time I came to see him, he asked me if I had ever gone to college, a question that never failed to astound me. Didn't I *look* like a college graduate? With my long, prematurely graying, dark curly hair, which I wore tied back into a thick braid, my penchant for flat leather sandals and 100 percent cotton blouses and billowing cotton skirts, I sometimes felt like a parody of an overeducated East Coast liberal. Then there was Harold. Harold was huge—*huge*—with arms and legs like rump roasts, hair like a helmet and shining with grease, trembling with barely contained outrage, mainly over how poorly the world had treated him. There was no real meanness in him, but you kind of had to tiptoe around him anyway. Little Chuck (who was called "Little Chuck" to distinguish him from Chuck Johnson, or "Big Chuck," the resident manager) was the only white guy in the joint and St. Anthony's most senior resident. He had had a successful catering company before he became ill, and like a lot of people in the food business, he loved not only to cook but to take care of other people, mother-hen style. He was, in his own words, a fairy—his bedroom stuffed with more tchotchkes than a gift shop, the walls plastered with lewd posters of half-naked men. Skinny and frail, covered with sores, and with wispy sandy hair and eyes made huge behind thick lenses, Little Chuck exerted a kind of pull on the others that far exceeded his physical presence. Moreover, with the possible exception of the caregivers, he knew more about what was going on than anyone else did. Who was sneaking alcohol. Who had spent the weekend smoking crack. Who was hiding potato chips in his room. Not that I knew anything about Little Chuck and his inside intelligence at the time, because Little Chuck made it clear that he had no use for me. When I went by his room to say hello or to ask him if there was anything I could do for him, he was polite, but no more than that.

So I turned my attentions to Geraldine. By the time I met her, Geraldine was already in the last stages of her disease and in hospice care, though you wouldn't necessarily have known it. Though the disease had whittled her away to practically nothing, she was pretty the way a bird is pretty, with small jutting bones under smooth skin and quick, darting movements. She had enormous eyes set in a wide face, sharp elbows, and a million stories about life on the edge, the picaresque that had been her grab-and-go existence in poor, black, struggling, segregated Baton Rouge. I'd sit on the edge of her bed while she told me about her former career as a check forger, her stay at a federal prison in Virginia, and the two stretches she did at the Louisiana State Penitentiary for Women. "Oh," she'd tell me, "we had us some good old times, we did indeed! Me and my old man, he was working delivering flowers, we'd start drinking beer around nine in the morning, keep going, have us a party in the back of that van! Just took the checks right out of folks' mailboxes, how they gon' catch us? We got those flowers in our hands. And easy to pull off, easy to cash, one nigger looks just like the rest to them folks at the bank. But in prison, I saw the light. Became a Christian. Confessed my sins and was washed clean. Jesus is good, oh Lord, he is good to me!"

Geraldine's room at St. Anthony's was spotless, with snapshots of her children and grandchildren thumb-tacked to the bulletin board and pastel curtains hanging in the one window. Her clothes hung neatly in the closet: the good things—her dresses and suits—in bright, happy colors, orange and pink and yellow, the shoes lined up below. Every morning she made her bed. She was fifty-four, and the first black person born in Baton Rouge General Hospital. Her mother had been working there, on the janitorial staff, when her water broke and couldn't make it to the charity hospital in New Orleans in time: someone had taken pity on her, permitting her to stay. "I made history," Geraldine liked to say.

As the months wore on she became gaunt—skeletal, even, her cheek-bones hyper-prominent, her eyes enormous, patches of her scalp showing through the scant hair on her head, toothless—but she never acted like a sick person, let alone one who was dying. She bristled with impatient energy; her eyes sparkled; she bragged about her adventures. At one point she asked me how many men I'd slept with before I met my husband. I told her that that was none of her business.

A few weeks before she died, Geraldine insisted that I drive her to her auntie's house (an "auntie" need not be your aunt by blood but rather an older, maternal woman for whom you have special affection) to deliver a box of clothing that Geraldine had been keeping for her own lover, the "old man" with whom she used to celebrate the successful forging of a check by drinking beer in the middle of the morning. He was in a coma in the public hospital, but, she said, eventually he'd need his things. She directed me through the sprawl of old South Baton Rouge; past sagging shotguns and the rusted-out shells of cars; past bramble bushes and empty lots filled with rotting boards, trash, and weeds; over the interstate; and past a gutted elementary school, whereupon Geraldine instructed me to hang two rights and a left, and we came to the place. The house was in a neighborhood straight out of an Eastern liberal's worst nightmare: sagging front porches, cardboard taped over broken windows, garbage and skinny dogs in the street, vacant-eyed young men huddling together wearing low-riding jeans and large gold jewelry. "You go, I ain't got no strength," Geraldine said as I pulled up. "Just tell Auntie that this from Geraldine. She'll know who you talking about."

So I left Geraldine—all ninety pounds of her—in the front seat of my car, hoisted the box into my arms, walked up to the door, and knocked. From across the street, a posse of young men watched me, their eyes huge with staring. I could feel them there, a weight at my back. They probably thought I was a social worker or a cop, but that didn't occur to me until months later. At the time, I only knew that they were over *there,* that I was standing on the front steps of a wretched shotgun in the middle of God knows where, and if I were shot and killed—shot and killed for my Ford minivan or perhaps for the pearl earrings that my parents had given me for my sixteenth birthday—no one would ever know, except perhaps for Geraldine, who didn't count and certainly couldn't protect me.

Auntie finally came to the door, opened it a crack, and after I explained what I was doing there, let me in. Inside, the stench was terrible: a combination of old dirt and rancid diapers and beer and rot and body odor, of generations of furtive couplings and freezing cold winters and broiling hot summers and not enough food and not enough light and no access and no way out. Or at least that's how it struck me. It was all I could do not to get sick. I stood there, trying not to gag, while Auntie gave me a long, cold stare. Behind her, there was a sagging sofa. Pictures of Jesus, blue-eyed and halo-lit, were tacked on the walls. Duct tape held the windows together. I wondered if I was going to make it out of there alive.

What was I doing there? I was raised in the suburbs, bred to decorate and play tennis and make my grandmother Helene's fabulous pot roast. I felt as self-conscious as when my mother insisted on calling me Jen Hen Rooster Dooster in front of my friends. Auntie looked me up and down and indicated that I was to put the box in the corner. I did as instructed, went back outside, drove Geraldine back to St. Anthony's, saw her back to her room, and said goodbye. "See you next week," I said, relieved beyond belief to be returning to my own life, my own little sliver of the safe, regular, calm, vacuumed, disinfected, and Pledge-dusted world. I was shocked when, a week later, I returned to St. Anthony's only to be told that Geraldine had died the night before. Her relatives were in her room, throwing her belongings into Glad bags.

Gerald was next. He died in May 1999. He was in his mid-thirties, from Sunshine, Louisiana, and his country accent was so thick, and he spoke so quickly, that I could barely understand him. His legs were useless, two heavy sacks of unmoving infection — *polyradiculopathy* — his sight was failing — *CMV-related retinitus* — there were days when he was certain that angels had visited him the night before and days when he swore that the mother of his one son, a pretty woman who had died a year or so earlier, also from AIDS, had beckoned him from heaven — *cranial nerve palsies, nystagmus, ataxia.* "I'm going to a better place," he told me over and over, and one day he gestured me over to his bedside and confided that he himself was an angel. "I saw an angel come right through that there window," he said, indicating the room's one window with a tilt of his head. "And you know what else? I's the angel."

"You're the angel?"

"I am the angel," he said. "The angel, he told me. He said, 'You is the angel, Gerald. You the angel.'"

Sure thing, I thought, but I came to his room anyway, came to him because he was so enormously sweet, so lovable, so unlike anyone I'd ever met before, completely open in a childlike way, without even a hint of bitterness or rancor, and anyhow, it wasn't Gerald's fault that he was hallucinating. God alone knew what the virus was doing to his synapses, his neurons and hippocampus and amygdala and sulci. If he wanted to believe that he was an angel, who was I to challenge him?

I read him the 23rd Psalm, Paul's second letter to the Thessalonians, Daniel in the lion's den. I read stories about Jesus' miracles and how he ascended to heaven. The stories left me dry, though; when I read them, I felt like a fraud, conscious that I couldn't read them the way Gerald would have preferred them being read — with a rich, melodious Southern rhythm, the call-and-response of the country church, with the women swaying to the beat of the preacher's preaching, and the men sweating in their Sunday best. Me, I sounded like a cross between Jerry Seinfeld and Ruth Bader Ginsburg. Gerald always thanked me anyhow.

Some time that winter, Gerald fell in love with Sheila, the cleaning lady. Unfortunately, another man, Nathaniel, was also in love with her, and he had a car. True, the car didn't work, but that didn't keep Nathaniel from washing it to a high shine, gazing at it longingly.

Before he'd gotten sick, Nathaniel had worked as a garbage man for the city of Baton Rouge; he'd contracted HIV from a blood transfusion. He supported an ex-wife and several children on his salary, and whenever he had any spare money he'd ask me to go take him to buy things for them: Pampers or jars of peanut butter or, once, a large black doll in a stiff yellow dress like the icing on a cupcake. Now he and Gerald were competing for the attentions of Sheila, who humored them both, spending time first with the one and then with the other, laughing at their jokes, fussing at them to take care of themselves, teasing and being teased. For a while, it seemed like Nathaniel had the clear edge, as not only was he up and on his feet but he was also a nice-looking man with beautiful, jet-black skin, a strong neck, long, tapering fingers, and an elegant shape, as if, once upon a time, he'd been a modern dancer. But he was shy and didn't talk much, whereas Gerald, bedridden, never shut up. Just before Easter, Gerald handed me his wallet and instructed me to go and buy the biggest, nicest Easter bunny I could find. There were hundreds of them at the Wal-Mart. The one I selected was pink, with enormous, sticking-up white ears, and when he presented it to Sheila, she blushed and everyone else clapped and stood around grinning, enjoying the wonderful spectacle of Gerald's love.

By the time Gerald died, in June of 1999, he'd been visibly failing for weeks: he could no longer see anything but shadows, his face had taken on an empty look, and he dozed with his sightless eyes open. By then I'd been coming to St. Anthony's for almost a year. A few hours before he died, and though I no longer thought that Gerald was present to hear me, I went to his room, sat with him, and then, as I got up to go, told him I'd be back to see him again. Which I knew was a flat-out lie. His breathing was labored, his chest making an empty rattling sound that later I was to learn is the death rattle that the body makes as it struggles to take in just one more breath, just one more beat of blood and bone. He died that afternoon while I was at home doing laundry or checking my e-mail or worrying about my career or obsessing about why on earth anyone would actually want to read *Tuesdays with Morrie* when anyone with even half a brain cell should know that it was worthless sentimental tripe. I didn't even go to Gerald's funeral in Sunshine because at the time I was trying to promote my first, just-published book and my publisher had set up a phone interview with a writer from a woman's magazine on the morning that Gerald was being laid to rest. I was so desperate for success that I probably would have missed my own mother's funeral if it had meant a chance on the Oprah show or an interview with *People*. And then Nathaniel died, too. Just took sick one day and landed in Earl K. Long Hospital with a raging fever, and the next thing I knew he was gone and in his room was a single light, like the electric Yahrzeit candles that Jews put out on the anniversary of a loved one's death, and no one talked about him anymore except to say that he'd gone to a better place.

Then Tommy, the math teacher, left—packing his bags, putting on a pair of well-pressed slacks, a stylish shirt, and shined shoes, and moving back to New Orleans, where a teaching job was awaiting him. Harold was doing well, too—so well that he was able to move into an apartment of his own. Which meant that from the original batch of twelve people who were at St. Anthony's when I started, just Little Chuck was left. Bit by bit, though, he'd started talking to me, asking me to take him places, telling me about his friends and family, and finally giving me bits and pieces of his life story. He told me that he preferred living at St. Anthony's to moving back home, to Fort Worth, because though he loved his parents, they drove him crazy. He gave me weekly T-cell count reports, dished dirt, told me who, among his friends in the restaurant business, had cocaine habits and who merely drank to excess, described the annual gay men's ball, and advised me to dye my hair, because, as he put it, being gray before forty wasn't nice. All this—the teasing, the hanging out, the stories—was a big deal for me. For the first time since I'd started volunteering at St. Anthony's, I felt like maybe my being there had a point.

"Oh, sweetheart," Lorraine now says in her lisping, Southern, singsongy voice as I swing the minivan into the parking lot at St. Anthony's, bringing me back again—back to this hot sticky late-October day in 2001, back to the tar shimmering in the heat, the sounds of insects dancing in the scrubby field where no one ever goes, though in the spring and summer it's filled with wildflowers and tall long grasses smelling of your childhood. "I love you."

"I love you too, Lorraine," I say, though I don't mean it. I don't love Lorraine at all. Not even a tiny bit. The people I love—truly love—are few, and Lorraine barely scratches the surface. And yet when she opens her mouth and sings along to the theme from *The Queen Latifah Show* or, even better, lets loose with a gospel number—her voice rich and flowing and mellow, a river of melted chocolate running through her vocal cords— every cell in my being vibrates.

Children, go where I send thee. How shall I send thee? I will send you one by one . . .

"See you next week, Lorraine," I say, jumping back in my minivan, finding the NPR station, heading for home.

As a child growing up in McLean, Virginia—the same cushy suburb where Robert F. Kennedy's family lived and where Kenneth Starr, to the outraged disgust of my mother, later made his home—I didn't know anyone, either Christian or Jewish, who professed any kind of real faith. The only person who even came close was Mae Carter, our Baptist maid, but she parked her religion, along with the oversized pocketbook that she always carried, at the back door, and never spoke about such matters at all, at least not in my presence.

Occasionally, on nights when my parents were out, Mae did remind me to say my bedtime prayers. I'd recite aloud a simple prayer that my father had composed, asking God to bless our family and help make me a good child—and then, after Mae had turned off the lights, I'd add one or two requests of my own that were far more fervent. I was a fearful, lonely, anxious child, convinced that my father, a lawyer, was almost mortally disappointed in me, and prone to stomachaches so severe that by the time I was in the sixth grade I was practically living on Maalox. Every night I begged God to spare me and my loved ones, including the dogs, from any number of calamities, each of which I would have to name, individually, in order to deflect the otherwise inevitable doom. But no one knew about my silent nightly ritual—surely no one would have understood it—and as I grew older I dropped it. It was useless, and worse, stupid and embarrassing; and in any event, I was busy.

And so the pattern continued as I grew up, went to college, moved to New York to work in publishing, married, became a mother, and reluctantly moved back to Washington, where I grew my own vegetables, learned to make pesto, and developed a passion for gleaming hardwood floors and tribal rugs. No one in our circle, even among the church- and synagogue-goers, even among the most rigorously observant, was truly a person of faith, by which I mean a person who counts God among his inner circle. At most, there were attempts made to keep certain traditions up, to educate children in the vocabulary of their faith traditions: baby naming ceremonies and bar and bat mitzvahs for the Jews, baptism and the occasional Mass for the Catholics, confirmation for Episcopalians. But all of this, it seemed, was done in accordance with a sense that passing the old forms down to the next generation was a good thing in and of itself, a kind of psychological bonding ritual intended to make one feel secure. As for God: He was merely a fairy tale.

Then Stuart took a job as a professor at LSU in Baton Rouge and we moved, with our three young children, to the Bible Belt, where just about anything that happens is attributed to the will of God. And not only by ministers: my friends and neighbors all tend to speak of their personal struggles in terms of God's will and their own talents and strengths in terms of divinely given gifts. The former governor got on the radio one summer and ascribed the rains that had finally broken a long drought to the power of prayer. True, he was a moron, but the point is that no one blinked an eyelash, either when he first asked Louisianans to pray for rain or when he proffered his explanation for how the rains eventually arrived.

It was all very new to me, but I must admit I rather liked it. My rational mind kept telling me that God, particularly for people like Lorraine who find themselves in a world of trouble, is nothing more than a security blanket. This is the God Who forgives you every last nasty thing you've ever done, and all you have to do ask. So you've killed a few folks? No problem! Just call on Him at the very end and—presto!—you get into heaven. Whored around? Don't sweat it! Cheated on your income taxes? Come on down! Still, on the whole, I felt more at ease among the faithful in Baton Rouge than I had among the earnestly well-meaning and extremely ambitious Ivy-educated lawyers and doctors and policy wonks and journalists who had made up our world in Washington. I liked the idea that God cared—liked it better than the idea that He was no more than a big sop for those who couldn't take reality or, alternatively, that if He did exist, it was in some way that was beyond human comprehension. At St. Anthony's, not only did He exist, but also, at times, He came down to earth to say howdy or give a thumbs-up. He was so present, so everyday, that you almost expected to bump into Him at the grocery store.

I'd been volunteering for about a year when my first book, *Food and Whine,* was finally published, to rave reviews from my closest friends and family and almost utter silence elsewhere. I'm exaggerating: the book actually sold a respectable number of copies, and in Baton Rouge, people made a big fuss over me. I was disappointed, though, having fully expected to hit the best-seller lists along with *Tuesdays with Morrie* and *Diana: Her True Story.* Still, the attention I did get I loved: I loved the reading I had at the Baton Rouge Barnes and Noble, I loved the articles about me in the local newspapers, and most of all I loved this wonderful feeling of having, at long last, made my mark, with a big-time New York publisher and a glossy, well-designed book jacket, the real thing, too, and not some fly-by-night no-name printing press for lesbian separatist want-to-be poets or political refugees from countries that no longer exist. It was this sense of having finally arrived, with a veritable, in-your-face, concrete success, that no one could take away. What a thrill! Only it was the thrill of an addict coming off a high and desperate for his next fix. The way it went for me, more or less, was this: *I'll show them.* Or rather: *My book will show them. Let's see them call me stupid once I've got a best seller and a date to appear on the David Letterman show.* Really. I'd somehow just *assumed* that by dint of my own desperation, my book would be such an utter and amazing success that I'd be snatched away from the realm of ordinary, messy, average humanity and placed in the pantheon of the gods, where not only would I finally be free of the kind of crushing dread and garden-variety self-hatred that had haunted me my entire life, but also, I'd be verifiably superior. *I'll show them!* The *them,* in this case, being, first, my large extended family of hyper-successful lawyers and businessmen and academics who had made me feel like I was nuts to begin with and, second, everyone from elementary school onward who had ever been mean to me. The only thing was, in order to continue riding the wave of my enormous success, I'd need a second book.

So I began what turned out to be the hopeless task of writing a follow-up (working title: *How's Bayou?*). I wrote like mad—the words simply flying out my fingers as I sat at my computer and typed. The only problem was, the more I wrote, the worse the book became. I was drowning. Drowning in a pile of stale, sticky, stupid verbiage. Then I turned forty. That week, when I walked into St. Anthony's on my usual day, everyone was sitting around the lounge, wearing shiny dark-green paper party hats, waiting for me. Little Chuck had planned the party, making a peach-torte birthday confection in my honor. As I sat on the sofa in the lounge, he placed it before me, and while everyone sang the "Happy Birthday" song, I made a wish and blew out the candles. Only I don't remember what I wished for. I like to think that I wished for healing—for the people at St. Anthony's, as well as for my own broken self—but what's more likely is that I asked for a book review in the *New York Times*. I put my usual two or three hours in, and then went home. And shortly thereafter, while on summer vacation in Maine with my family, I had what I can only call a crisis of faith.

It was a very physical thing. Sitting under the gorgeous arching blue sky, smelling the pine-scented air, listening to the birds call to each other, watching my three children play hide-and-seek among the trees, all tanned and freckled like in a Gap ad, I felt my faith, never strong to begin with, leak out of me like milk out of a smushed-up carton in the back of the car. I felt it in my chest, where my heart tightened up into a hard little nugget, angry and mean, slit-eyed and fulminating, and I felt it in my extremities, which suddenly seemed filled with something tingly and stinging—some existentialist Pepsi-Cola, mixed, perhaps, with acid. I'd had anxiety attacks all my life, but this one felt different and more threatening.

Though I'd always struggled with Judaism, I'd never really left it, and I thought I knew enough about it to know that, at least on one level, it doesn't require of you an absolute and constant belief in God—a quality that I'd always found vastly comforting. Rabbi Paul Caplan, who was our rabbi in Baton Rouge when we first arrived, liked to talk about Jews as "God wrestlers," in the sense in which the patriarch Jacob in the Bible wrestled with the angel and thereby earned his new name, Israel—meaning, as the angel informs him, "You have wrestled with God and with man and prevailed." Being a Jew in this sense means having a kind of divine permission to argue with the divine itself. Or as our current, and much beloved Baton Rouge rabbi, Stan Zamek, was fond of saying: God is bigger than religion. But I was sweating buckets anyhow—the rivulets were pouring down my ribs and landing in the waistband of my newly purchased J. Crew walking shorts. My entire body shook with fear.

It's such a cliché that I'm embarrassed to admit it, but my immediate crisis in faith came about courtesy of Darwin, that old joker. He had never bothered me before, even when I was a child and used to stare, fixated, at the drawings in the *World Book Encyclopedia* of man evolving from the apes. So we emerged from the trees: what of it? In my own private cosmology, that hardly meant that God hadn't, somehow or other, also created us and breathed into our souls some yearning to reach Him. I just didn't think about it too hard. But now, in Maine, I was doing nothing but thinking about it, and my problems were magnified by my reading of Steven Pinker's *How the Mind Works.*

What I got out of this book—which I struggled with on the hammock in the shade of the pine trees, reading and then rereading paragraphs—was that we human beings had been fashioned by the forces of evolution to have minds capable of postulating God. Or, to put it another way, the ability to conceive of God was programmed into our common human hard drive over hundreds of millions of years and now served, along with our ability to make art and compose Budweiser jingles, as the outer limit of those qualities of higher intelligence that gave our species such a ridiculous edge to begin with.

It made sense. On the other hand, it was awful, even obscene. Because a world without God—even for someone like me who had never been dead-certain that He existed in the first place—was a much lonelier place than a world set in the palm of His hand. And also, from a Jewish point of view, if God didn't exist, then the mitzvoth, or commandments, starting with the Big Ten and moving on up through laws informing every aspect of life, including the commandment to visit the sick, ultimately meant nothing. If God was only a figment of our flimsy yearnings, why bother? I felt cheated, like a fool who'd fallen for the biggest Lothario of all.

One evening, I sat with Stuart and my father under the miraculous dome of the sky—that wonderful northern star-spangled sky undimmed by pollution or city lights—trying to sort things out. Unfortunately, my husband, whose style of perception is highly cerebral, basically doesn't believe in God at all and therefore wasn't all that well equipped to reassure me in matters of belief. He's a classic neck-up kind of guy and even looks the part: with a high, smooth forehead, enormous dark eyes, silver-gray hair, and an elegant, elongated figure. Complete strangers, meeting him for the first time, have no trouble guessing that he's a college professor, although as far as I'm concerned, he'd do better as a Lands' End model. (I picture him in the role of the distinguished white-haired guy leaning on the fireplace, wearing a teal-colored crewneck of 100 percent lamb's wool.) For him, God is a nice idea, but not much more than that: it's Judaism itself that he cares about, both for its ethical teachings and its magnificent, world-changing, tragic and terrible history. As for my father, he is an inveterate synagogue-goer and had raised me and my siblings on stories of the happy days, back in his hometown of Baltimore, where Jews were really Jews, none of this namby-pamby non-Hebraic ethics-only Judaism for him, may as well throw the damn baby out with the damn bathwater. And yet Dad also didn't snuggle up to God on any regular basis. In fact, as a family, we had never talked about Him at all. We talked about Israel. We talked about What Was Good for the Jews. We talked about anti-Semitism. The rest of my extended family had long since abandoned any kind of serious practice of religion at all, and though her views had softened somewhat in the wake of her illness, my mother's long-held belief was that both God and religion were, in a word, "crap."

"Dad," I finally said, "I'm having a little difficulty with God." We had had a wonderful dinner, and as we sat there under the brilliant bright stars I told him about Pinker, and how suddenly I felt both lonely and unhinged, for if there was no ultimate moral center of things then everything we call ethical was no more than a human confection. I don't know exactly what kind of assurances I expected to get out of this encounter, particularly as most of my struggles with Judaism in particular and life in general sprung from the totally weird way in which my father had raised me, but I was hoping at the very least to be pointed in another direction, to be shown an error in my thinking that might itself point to bigger possibilities.

Dad leaned back, gazed at the stars, and said: "I've personally never believed in any particular conception of God, although I've found it fascinating to study how religious thinkers have grappled with the notion of the divine over the centuries, and I suggest you read, for starters, Maimonides." He continued in this vein for a while, and then—in an effort, I suppose, to make me feel better—said that if God Himself came down from the heavens to proclaim that He didn't exist, he, my father, wouldn't change his way of life by one iota. "I'd continue going to shul," he said, "I'd continue observing Shabbat, I'd continue studying Jewish history, metaphysics, and law, and I'd continue to embrace Jewish communal life—because, Jennifer, the Jewish tradition itself has inherent value, with or without God."

Which was all fine and good, but didn't help. And why was I going to my father for help anyway? He and I had never come close to understanding each other, let alone sharing a sensibility or instinctive sympathy borne of familial ties. After all, this was the same father who, when I came to him bawling one day because some kids at school had told me that I was ugly, comforted me by explaining that though I may at present be somewhat homely, Jewish girls tended to hold onto their looks, whereas non-Jews don't. "Blondes fade," is how he put it. Two years later, he insisted that I walk alone in the winter dawn darkness through the woods to catch the school bus, refusing to let my mother drive me, on the theory that he wanted me to be self-reliant, which wouldn't have been so bad had a girl around my age not just been hacked to pieces by a madman a couple of miles down the road. And so forth. And now I was going to him for solace over the loss of God? As if my father, who had hardly been an ace in the comfort department when I was a child, and was now in his seventies, burdened with worries about my mother, could restore to me the God of Abraham, Isaac, and Jacob? The God Who led the children of Israel out of Egypt? The God Who spoke through the prophets, imploring Israel to repent and return? The God Who loved Israel above all other nations? The God Who commanded "Justice, justice shall you pursue" and "Do not oppress the stranger, the widow, and the orphan"? I felt like the Little Prince, up there on his lonely planet in the middle of the vast cosmos. Stuart counseled me to get to work again as soon as possible, saying that things would begin to make sense as soon as I was back at my computer. But this avenue seemed choked off, too: for me, writing and praying had always been complementary activities, a kind of working out, in words, of the story I wanted my soul to tell. But now the words themselves seemed meaningless—an endless stream of monkey chatter.

The house my parents built in Maine is very beautiful, airy and open, perched above a lake like a ship at sea, creating the illusion that water is actually passing beneath it, whereas in reality it's half a football field away. But it has one architectural detail that I find both strange and disturbing. In each of the two front rooms, the floor-to-ceiling windows are designed in a geometric pattern, starting with a wide base, and then tapering to a single square of glass under the V of the ceiling. Embedded in the design is the shape of an enormous cross. You don't always notice the crosses, but at night, if you close the curtains in the front bedroom, where Stuart and I sleep, the crosses pop out like emblazoned rallying cries—or like those figures hidden in the "Magic Eye" page of the comics, impossible to discern until you see them, and then equally impossible not to discern. All the rest of that difficult summer, I'd lie in bed gazing at the giant cross made by the curtained windows and think: *What is God trying to tell me?* But then I'd remember that there is no God—just my own relentless yearning.

When St. Anthony's first opened its doors in 1986, most of its residents were gay: AIDS was then primarily a disease of homosexual men. But since then the face of the crisis had changed, and in Baton Rouge, as in much of the South, it was growing fastest among drug abusers, whites as well as blacks, and affecting equal numbers of men and women. St. Anthony's had twelve bedrooms for residents, and at the time of my own crisis it was staffed at the top by Chuck Johnson in the role of chief administrator and Dolly Williams as social worker; but the people who really ran the show and knew what was going on were Joanna and Caroline and Martha and Grace, the caregivers, who typically worked in teams of two. These were the people who brushed the patients' hair and cleaned up their messes and wiped their spittle and blood and held their hands and said, "I love you," and "Jesus loves you," and "Make damn sure you're taking your medication because if you don't you'll never get better and don't you know that we love you and we don't want you to die. Jesus is good, yes he is, there you go, drink all that juice, it's good for you!" They fussed and cajoled, wheedled and begged, and generally loved you up, no matter how recalcitrant, obnoxious, ungrateful, or downright repulsive you were.

Depending on the season, too, there were particular residents who, by virtue of either duration or their own leadership qualities, were "senior" in the eyes of staff and other patients alike—people to whom all would turn for help. When I started volunteering at St. Anthony's, in October 1998, the person in this position was Little Chuck. And when I returned from our summer vacation in Maine, Little Chuck, though so thin he had practically disappeared, was still Queen Bee. Had we gone to any good restaurants? Had I heard that Big Chuck was thinking about going back to school to get a degree in nursing? And what about that new resident—the young one with the bad teeth—Ieesha? Doesn't even know she's got AIDS, let alone how she got it. It's so pathetic it makes you want to weep.

What could I say? I was hardly happy to be back in Baton Rouge, where I'd once again have to face my hopelessly awful manuscript. ("Alligators aren't kosher, but, like Chinese takeout, they aren't exactly *treyf* either.") Come to think of it, I wasn't exactly crazy about being among the dying and the desperate at St. Anthony's either, no matter what kind of baloney I told myself about what the prophets say about taking care of the widow and the orphan. After all, the people at St. Anthony's weren't widows or orphans, and nowhere in all of Jewish writ does a single rabbi, prophet, or commentator so much as mention the word *AIDS*. But ever since my birthday, I felt that I'd passed through a gate and couldn't go back. No matter how badly I might be suffering from lack of faith, or how bored I might be as I schlepped around Baton Rouge in search of discount Kools or Little Debbie chocolate-fudge brownies—the kind in the blue box, not the kind in the pink box—I believed I couldn't quit, that doing so would have constituted a failure, if not of my own sense of ethics, then of imagination, which in some ways was worse.

Still, I can't really claim that when I got back to St. Anthony's after vacation I felt like a complete and utter fraud, although I suppose that, to the extent that I pretended sympathy to the notion of Jesus as physician and read psalms of praise, I was. But it was too late for simply claiming fraudhood and moving on. It was more like I felt an odd sense of disconnect, which was only heightened by my fistfight with Steven Pinker. On any given day, I was present at conversations that centered on death and overcoming death through Jesus, and as a resident held my hand or let me give her a Kleenex, the assumption was that I, too, was on the Jesus boat. But I wasn't, and now I wasn't even sure that I believed in any kind of God, by any name, at all.

The new resident didn't help my mood much, either. Ieesha was only twenty or twenty-one but already visibly dying: she was covered with sores, her hands trembled, her feet were swollen, and her eyes bled ooze. Nevertheless, she hung on, terrified of dying, demanding, whiny, and, as far as I could tell, utterly ignorant of what was happening to her, or why. And what *had* happened to her, I wanted to know. She had at least one child, a little girl: How had *that* happened? Had she been raped or merely knocked up? Her teeth stuck out of her head at odd angles: Had she been beaten? Her hair, what was left of it, grew in clumps. Her family, or what family she had, never visited, or even called, though she did have a grandmother who occasionally sent her money. Who had raised her? Or hadn't Ieesha been raised at all? I was dying to ask, but couldn't, because in point of fact I don't think that anyone on staff knew what her history was either.

Seeing myself in a maternal role, I tried to like her, or at least feel for her, but the truth is, I didn't like her one bit. She didn't exactly like me, either. I know this because every time I said hello to her, she looked at me as if I were a piece of rancid meat. Nevertheless, she'd ask me to take her to the shopping mall. I would push her along in her wheelchair, and she would complain that I was going too fast or too slow. If I took her to Sears, she decided she wanted to go to J. C. Penney's. If I got her to Penney's, she didn't like the merchandise. When I told her that I had to get going, she'd begin to cry. I'd apologize, wheedle, coax. I felt like slapping her.

One day, she insisted that I take her out to buy a new pair of shoes, and we ended up at one of those giant discount athletic-shoe stores that sell a seemingly endless variety of different brands, a huge box of a place marooned on the outer edge of the shopping mall's interior ring road. Ieesha's grandmother, apparently, had just sent her one hundred dollars in new twenty-dollar bills. The only problem was that Ieesha's feet were so swollen that she could barely walk. The salesman, a young, handsome man with an athletic swagger, who couldn't have been much older than Ieesha herself, brought out first one pair, and then the next, and then the next, none of which were exactly right, exactly what Ieesha wanted. He flashed confidence and ease, and Ieesha just kept looking at him with her enormous, yellow eyes. Finally she began to flirt with him, and he—perhaps out of kindness—flirted back. Just a little, just enough to put her at her ease, just enough so that, in the end, after trying on and then discarding a dozen or more pairs, she bought herself some running shoes. They were blue, with light blue stripes, and cost more than eighty dollars. I wanted to weep. Then she wanted to go to another store to buy a track suit—this for a girl who couldn't walk—but by then I had had enough. "I have another job I have to get back to," I said, thinking of my dreadful book—the one that was getting worse and worse with every additional sentence. "And anyway, we've been out for more than two hours, it'll be lunchtime soon."

"You so mean to me," she said. "You so damn mean all the time." Tears slid down her face. "What you looking at?" she said. Then she clammed up and gazed out the window, her face set resolutely away from me. Meanwhile, I decided to rescue the situation by engaging in light, pleasant conversation, chattering away about all kinds of stupid, meaningless shit—the weather, the cost of housing, the green sofa that had recently been replaced in the lounge at St. Anthony's—and as I chattered away, I watched myself become progressively idiotic. I couldn't stop myself, though, and continued chattering away all the way back to St. Anthony's, where I unbuckled her, helped her out of my minivan, and half-carried, half dragged her inside. By the time Ieesha was safely deposited back in her room, I felt like I'd been whittled down to the bone.

But Joanna, the caregiver on duty that morning, told me: "Don't take no crap from her, Jennifer. You the one doing her the favor. You don't need to take no lip." Of course she was right, and she ought to have known. Joanna herself had been working at St. Anthony's for years, doing whatever she thought it took, at any given time, to help, and she herself did not take crap, under any circumstances. "You treat me nice, and I'll treat you nice," I'd heard her say, more than once, to more than one uncooperative resident. Or: "You think Jesus wouldn't take his medicine? You better get down on your knees and thank your savior that you got this medicine that most people can't afford, and then you pick up that glass of water and take those pills." Built like a linebacker, with strong legs and hips, and a small oval face under a short, tight hairstyle, at first Joanna didn't strike me as being any kind of angel of mercy, but rather, a drill sergeant or perhaps a counselor at a tough-love boot camp for juvenile delinquents: brusque, no-nonsense, and unfeeling. But the reverse was true: Joanna—as I came to learn—was a tzaddik, a holy person. Everyone loved her, and more often than not, Joanna's would be the last face that a dying resident saw. When Ieesha died, in late October, she was surrounded not by her own family—who had been absent the entire length of her stay—but by Joanna, Caroline, and Little Chuck, who had, just a few weeks earlier, given her a bottle of perfume.

And now the deaths kept coming. Thomas, who had lost his eyesight to AIDS but insisted on walking back and forth in the parking lot, walking until he felt solid on his feet again, died in November. Donny, a raggedy-haired white guy with tattoos all over his body and a whole set of racist assumptions, went into the bathroom one morning to brush his teeth and never came out. In his spare time, he'd like to do leatherwork, making fabulously intricate belts, mainly for his mother. A very pretty young woman with café-au-lait skin and two young children moved into Ieesha's old room and died the next day. Pody died. Kevin died. Ernest died. Tommy, who had resumed his teaching duties in New Orleans, had taken sick again, dying at his sister's house in Baton Rouge. Word filtered through. Some more people, whose names I can't even remember, died. I didn't understand it. What was the point?

"They all going to a better place," Joanna said. Sure they were. "You just got to believe," Joanna said. But I didn't, and I certainly didn't believe in the beautiful fairy tale of heaven, or in the other strange notion that was taken for granted at St. Anthony's—that death wasn't a failure, but rather represented a triumph, insofar as it meant that the departed was now free to return to God. "Going home" is how people at St. Anthony's described death. But for me, death was just death: the end of the line, the cessation of all meaning, hope, love, and goodness. Utter and complete nothingness, stretching on for forever. Death—the thing you spent your whole life trying to avoid. There was no solace, and I just kept sinking deeper and deeper into this awful feeling that my whole life, and indeed all of human endeavor, was basically no more than a nasty practical joke.

"It's okay, faith is difficult," Rabbi Stan finally said to me one day when I cornered him in the synagogue parking lot and told him about my crisis of the summer. He added: "The struggle itself is the proof that you're in relationship to the divine." But I didn't buy it.

Then, in the spring, Little Chuck died. He had broken his hip in December and landed in the hospital with a high fever and a raging infection. One day I drove a couple of the other residents up to see him at Baton Rouge General, and when we got there, we found Joanna—who was on her day off—at his side. She was reminding him to count his blessings: her eyes were locked onto his, and her love for him—a love that didn't seem particularly personal—filled the room. Little Chuck stayed in the hospital for almost a month before finally coming back to St. Anthony's to die. He lay in his bed, under his quilts, in traction, with all those lustful come-hither, half-naked men gazing down upon him. His T cells had been virtually nonexistent for more than two years. He had thrush, hairy leukoplakia, gingivitis, diarrhea, seborrheic dermatitis, fungal infections, retinitus. He died holding Joanna's hand. The last words out of his mouth were "I love you."

Shortly after Little Chuck's death, Joanna asked me whether I was planning to write any more books. I told her that I hoped to, but that the whole enterprise was complicated—agents, contracts, what's fashionable and what's not, blah blah blah. Basically, I told her nothing, partly out of a defensive attitude that I've developed over the years in an effort to ward off bad karma (so if you're a writer, how come I've never heard of you?) and partly because, in my experience, most people don't really understand that writing is more than a hobby. How could I tell her that yes, I was working on another book, but that since my crisis of faith I'd felt so dry inside that the words weren't flowing, and that, even if they were, I was having problems with my agent—who wasn't returning my phone calls and hence made me feel like a geeky freshman girl with a crush on the high-school quarterback—and that even if I could manage to straighten things out with her and get all my work done, it was entirely possible that not one single publisher would be interested in my book? And why should they be, anyway, given that the book sucked? My own mother didn't really understand what I did; what could I expect from Joanna?

But she was not put off. "When you sit down to write, what do you do? Use a computer?" she said.

"Yes."

"You ask God to help you out?"

"No."

"Why not?"

I stammered something along the lines of how I felt it was selfish to ask God to help me write when there were so many more serious problems in the world. Thinking: any God who cares about my career isn't the kind of God I want running things.

"Nothing's too small for God," Joanna said. "He is the Creator, isn't He? And He gave you a gift of creativity, didn't He? Why wouldn't He want you to use it?"

The next time I sat down in front of my computer, I tried it. I closed my eyes, bent my head, and asked God to help me tap whatever gifts I possessed. I felt stupid, and in any event God didn't answer. The screen lay blank before me. I watched the dust motes dancing in the sunshine. I wrote a paragraph, then deleted it. I logged onto AOL and messed around on the web for a while. I e-mailed some friends. I checked to see if any of them had e-mailed me back. Then I had lunch.

The next day was no better, or the next. When I returned to St. Anthony's the following week Joanna asked whether I'd come to my senses and asked God for help.

"Actually, yes," I said.

"Good. What He say back?"

"Nothing."

"He will," Joanna said. "Give Him time. He'll let you know when He's ready."

"I don't think so."

Joanna was silent for a few moments, then she looked at me and said, "Not everyone ready for God. But He gives us different gifts. He needs me, but, see, He needs you, too. You a good person, Jennifer. You a good person." And off she went to tend to another new resident, Philomena. Philomena was originally from Nigeria, and once upon a time she'd been beautiful, but now her legs were so swollen that she could barely walk, and her face was bloated and puffy, like the Pillsbury Doughboy's. "Gotta get you into a nice hot bath," I heard from down the hall. "Help ease your pain, girl. We gonna try to ease that pain."

When Joanna came back, she asked again whether I would humble myself enough before the Lord to ask Him for help.

"I don't know," I said.

"How do you know unless you try?" Joanna said. "Got to give Him time."

So the next time I sat down to write, feeling like a fake, I called on the Lord to help me out as best He could.

"Dear Lord," I said, "Please allow me to use the gifts that You have given me." I didn't hear anything, but I went to work anyway, and this book is what I wrote.

2

The Dancing Widow

We moved to Baton Rouge in the summer of 1995, because my husband, a Washington lawyer, no longer wanted to be a lawyer. He wanted to be a law professor. When, in March of that year, he called me from his office to tell me that he'd landed a teaching job at LSU, my first thought was "Oh, dear God, no." My next thought was: "Well, at least we won't have to live there for very long." After all, I figured, it would only be a matter of time until he traded up: LSU would be a kind of starter job, a way station where Stuart would hone his scholarly skills for a better job at a better university in a better town: Ann Arbor, say, or Charlottesville. Because Baton Rouge was not my idea of a better town. I'd already been there once, on the occasion of his job talk, and once was enough. For starters, Baton Rouge is flat. Not flat the way New York is flat; it's *flat* flat, the biggest hills in the whole region the man-made levees that the Army Corps of Engineers built to hold back the Mississippi. Also, Baton Rouge is most definitely the South—the breeding grounds of George Wallace, David Duke (who almost won the governorship of Louisiana in 1991), Anita Bryant, and, for that matter, George W. Bush. It has mega-churches, giant white crosses looming over the interstate, and people who think that the ACLU is a satanic cult. I grew up in the sixties and seventies, worshipping the hippies who flocked to Washington to protest the Vietnam War and agitate for civil rights (and who, on occasion, landed in sleeping bags in our playroom in McLean, where they regaled us kids with stories about the wonderful visions they'd had while on acid). The South was the place you got away from—as indeed my mother's family had—not the place you went *to*. You went *to* New York, as I myself had done after college, and would have continued to do, had my husband not insisted that a New York law practice would have just about sucked his soul clear out of his body, leaving him an empty husk, a dried-out, desiccated former human being with nothing to show for his efforts other than a spacious prewar apartment on the Upper West Side, which, frankly, would have been just fine with me. And Baton Rouge wasn't even a real city, but—as my father helpfully put it when we announced the news of our upcoming move—an overgrown cow town, a sprawling metastasis of urban blight with big city problems and small town parochialism. The public schools are a disaster; the rate of AIDS transmission is the second-highest in the country; the murder rate is astronomical; there are serial killers, hurricanes, mosquitoes the size of your fist, and giant petrochemical plants ringing the city like monsters straight out of the book of Revelations, exhaling their fetid air into the night while you sleep and entering your membranes as you dream. Summers are so brutally hot that you feel like the end of the world is indeed nigh, fall never comes at all, and ignorance is considered to be a virtue. High school students drop to their knees to pray to Jesus before football games; right-wing groups organize boycotts against stores that instruct their employees to say "Happy Holidays" instead of "Merry Christmas"; and even people who know that you're Jewish tend to say things like, "What church did y'all say you go to?" As for the Jewish community itself—what Jewish community?

We moved a month before my twins turned two, leaving our lovely, leafy street in Northwest Washington, and our lovely, liberal, and earnestly good neighbors behind, for a chance at what I kept telling myself would be a simpler, more authentically lived life, whatever that meant. Despite my years of therapy, with a whole series of talented psychotherapists in varying shades of Freud, I was a bundle of neuroses, a walking, talking package of unresolved pain, a font of anxiety. My career seemed permanently stuck in the land of almost. I hated my father, except when I loved him. My only brother and I hadn't gotten along since I was four and he was three. My maternal grandmother, Jennie—the wondrous, magical, beautiful, and brilliantly charming grandmother after whom I'd been named—had had a series of small strokes that had left her living in the ever-constant present tense, unable to look after herself, prey to every shyster and cold-blooded con-artist in the English-speaking world, and had had to be moved from her airy house in Scarsdale, New York, to an institution in Connecticut with one of those names that sounds like a douche—Shady Pines, Whispering Elms. To top it all off, my beloved mother was just one month out of a chemotherapy regime that had left her bald, emaciated, and so nauseated that even on her good days she could barely lift her head from the pillow. Not that it had worked, either. She still had a visible tumor, which her doctors had pronounced inoperable. Additional chemo, in the meantime, would have killed her. As I boarded the airplane at Washington National for points south, my mother, who had always been so vigorous that it was practically obscene, was absorbing the news that for her there would be no respite from cancer, no remission, and certainly no cure. And I, her middle daughter—the one who, in the family mythology, had been born onto her team and who looked so much like her that I myself sometimes thought it was my mother, and not I, who was staring back at me from the mirror? I was flooded with relief, practically ecstatic at the thought of finally escaping her, liberating myself from her large personality. *Free at last!* It wasn't something I could talk about, and I never did discuss it with my mother until a full year after she died and she began to visit me in my dreams, but whenever I was with her, I felt my own personality, my own inner self, shrink and harden and begin to hiss, until there was nothing left of me but a wisp of smoke. But now I was getting free of all that. My mother cried buckets when I kissed her goodbye, packing my three small children into the waiting car and waving out the windows until I couldn't see her anymore. She cried until she was all cried out, and then she cried some more. She looked like a corpse.

We flew to Baton Rouge via Memphis. Beneath our plane, South Louisiana spread out as a patchwork of dull, marshy green, the Mississippi River appeared like a fat, chocolate-brown snake, the pilot announced our approach, and we landed. It was July.

My eldest child, Sam, then six, started first grade, Stuart started teaching, and I settled down—as much as I could with two-year-old twins in tow—to the serious business of showing everyone I met that I was smarter than they were, that I most definitely wasn't from Louisiana, or anywhere close to Louisiana, and that, in addition, I had no intention, ever, of attending an LSU football game. (I should have stuck to *this* resolution. The one time I went to a Tigers game, I was so certain that the entire stadium would soon collapse from the force of thousands of rabid Tigers fans stomping and cheering that I spent most of the game imagining our funerals.) The good news was that we'd been able to buy a big, old wooden house in the Garden District, near LSU, a neighborhood of huge spreading live oak trees, gardens overflowing with sweet william and old-growth azaleas, deep shade, screened-in porches, dogs, and a large number of gay men. And there in that house I'd sit, listening to the sound of the air conditioning humming through the vents, while first one twin and then the other spilled his or her dinner on the floor or spat up or cried or needed to be held or comforted or changed or bathed. I was so lonely that, as soon as I finally got Rose and Jonathan to stop crying, I myself would sit and weep, gazing out the window at the heartless, hard-baked green earth, while my babies looked at me with dark, astonished curiosity.

I did love the house, though. I loved the old, flowered wallpaper in the upstairs bedrooms—sprays of pink and yellow blooms that reminded me of the wallpaper in my grandmother's bedroom in Scarsdale. I loved the creaking floorboards that turned the color of honey in the afternoon sun, and the little back stairway that led from the kitchen directly to the master bedroom upstairs. I loved the magnolia trees in the front yard, and the live oaks in the back, and the sense of dwelling in safety and comfort, in a place with a story, a history all of its own. (Some time later we learned that our house had in fact been the staging ground of much of the political opposition to Huey P. Long.) What I didn't love was my overwhelming sense that life had left me behind, that I was buried alive, invisible, and worse, inconsequential, that my career, barely started, was already over, that I'd never again have friends, or if I did, they would be the kind of friends you make on your first day of college so you don't have to eat alone in the cafeteria. Plus it was hot: every time I ventured outside, I felt like I'd fallen into some terrifying, nameless, extra-terrestrial ooze. Stuart was ecstatic to be out of the law business and into the professor business, but I wasn't at all sure that this new turn my life had taken would work out. I'd sit in the front room, listening to my old James Taylor records with a baby or two on my lap, and fantasize about how, if I could only get the right kind of tribal rug for the living room, the exact right shade of off-white for the kitchen, and perhaps an antique cast-iron chandelier, life would do what I wanted, and my perfect surroundings would somehow melt into me, such that I too would experience metamorphosis, purification, beauty.

I've actually been prone to this particular misconception—shall we call it the Pottery Barn fallacy?—almost my entire adult life, and I blame my friend Nan for it. Nan was my best friend growing up in McLean, only her house, unlike ours, was not only remarkably free from clutter, mess, germs, mold, dirt, and dust, piles of naked plastic baby dolls in tin tubs on the patio (where my little sister liked to give them baths), armies of raggedy stuffed animals, and sprawling forts made out of a combination of blocks, shoeboxes, and sticks, but was also, unlike ours, decorated in classic High Wasp style, with old Oriental rugs on the hardwood floors, pastel-colored, slightly faded flowered bedspreads covering the four-poster beds, and small collections of seashells, brought back from summers on Cape Cod. Perched amid acres and acres of woods and fields at the top of a high hill, surrounded by Nan's mother's flower gardens and smelling like a combination of old leather and Pledge, Nan's house represented a magic that eluded me, a sense of order and privilege and ease that I, with my wildly curly dark brown hair, scrawny legs, inability to hit any ball whatsoever, middling grades, and stomachaches, could never attain. Compared to Nan, my own life, my own *self*, seemed cramped and humid, a breadbox filled with moldy bread. No matter that, soon after our tenth birthdays, Nan's parents announced that they were getting a divorce, her older sister developed a shoplifting habit, and her father's drinking problem blossomed into full-fledged alcoholism, whereas in my own family, we merely went quietly, and privately, nuts. I was certain that the key to happiness was to be found in home décor, and to this day I tend to suffer fits of decorating envy so severe that Stuart periodically threatens to cut off all my catalogs.

Despite my second career as a psychoanalytic patient (clutcher of Kleenex, rememberer of dreams), I have a hard time writing about my childhood. When I do, I feel like I'm hurtling toward a black hole, or like I'm remembering someone else's history, or tripping. Then I start to cry. And *then* I start to wonder why it is that in middle age I still insist on sifting through the little black burnt lumps and long-cold ashes of my long-ago childhood. What do I expect to discover, a corpse? *Oh look—there's the head! He looks just like Richard Nixon! How come I never noticed him before? And what's he doing in my formative years, anyway?* As my friend Megan once explained to me, the problem with my childhood—at least in terms of *story,* of coherent, dynamic *narrative*—isn't that it wasn't sufficiently miserable, but rather, that the players in it simply weren't monstrous enough to turn into compelling characters on the page. My parents were neither cruel nor crazy. In short—unlike my friend Debra, whose insanely vicious mother insisted that holding Debra's hand under scalding hot water was a salubrious way to "teach" her how to be "good"—I don't have any villains in my childhood baggage. The best I can come up with is a bunch of tattered, ill-fitting underwear.

My father was a lawyer. He was also, largely by virtue of having been born and raised in an Orthodox family in Baltimore, the Jew in the family—Baltimore being the place where Jews were really Jews, none of this namby-pamby Reform stuff, this watered-down, sissified modern Judaism-as-lifestyle crap that your mother was raised on, this lack of standards that, in turn, is creating an entire generation of ignorant know-nothings with their universal ethical views that didn't work in Europe under Hitler and won't work now, let me ask you, what happened to those German Jews who thought that their enlightened views of citizenship would bring about the full recognition of the equal rights of Jews as citizens of Europe? They went up in smoke, Jen, because without the particularism of Judaism, without its exacting demands, its rituals—our Shabbat, our dietary laws, our Torah, our language—the whole damn religion simply disappears, it simply melts away into the greater culture, which is exactly what you're seeing when you see Jews celebrating Christmas or having an organ in the synagogue. The organ is a Christian instrument, not a Jewish one. Jews sing without musical accompaniment. Everyone knows that.

And so it went, except not in any such sustained outburst, because the secret of my father—at least when I was growing up—was that he barely talked at all. Or at least not to us. He talked to his law partners, and to the ambassadors and undersecretaries, congressmen and policy wonks, with whom he played tennis and had lunch. He also talked, on occasion, to his older sister, whom he revered, and at times he must have talked to our mother too, although I never actually witnessed them talking about anything other than practical matters: where my older sister, Binky, should go to camp, or whether my brother, David, should have a math tutor. What he did was work. He got into his dark-green Thunderbird convertible and drove fifteen miles through thick, green wooded hills until he came to the Key Bridge, at which point he crossed into Washington, where he disappeared into the imposingly heavy facade on 16th Street, where his law firm was housed. The firm, then as now, was one of Washington's old-line, white-shoe law firms, its very hallways exuding restrained, refined power. It was the big time. It was the *big* big time: the land of the Ur-goy, the super-wasp, of Dean Acheson and McGeorge Bundy. My father always claimed that when he was hired, it was to fill one of the few "Jewish seats" in the firm, a spot that apparently had recently been vacated. Whatever the reasons, my father liked it there among the hushed cool hallways strewn with Oriental rugs, where, throughout my childhood, he toiled away day and night, among mounds of yellow legal pads and big, fat dull-as-death books with titles like *Corporate Mergers: 1950–1951*, and *Administrative Law: High Court Case Summaries*, ambitious, focused, and so determined to succeed that you could smell it on him, like a musk.

My mother, on the other hand, was neither Orthodox nor from Baltimore, had never learned the Hebrew alphabet, and loved lobster, Broadway musicals, and talking. The spirited second daughter of strikingly beautiful, cultured, and highly assimilated German Jews, my mother had grown up in Scarsdale, a place that, in our family, signified the perils of a certain kind of wealth, as the Jews there—again according to my father's way of thinking—did little more than play golf, decorate their gorgeous mansions, and ski. They were, in a word, "frivolous." (No matter that my parents would soon take up skiing themselves, or that my father eventually became something of a wine connoisseur and art collector.) Her childhood home was large and airy, with flower gardens, an apple orchard, a cook, a nanny, a driver, and scads and scads of the pastel-colored English chintz that my grandmother Jennie—who herself was so charming that it was impossible not to fall under her spell—loved. But no matter how elegant, no matter how charming or gracious or refined, my mother's family was

Reform—which is to say that they belonged to the modernized and least ritualistic sect of American Judaism—and therefore didn't rate. There was what my mother later called a "strong Jewish feeling," but there was no real attachment to the God of Israel, probably because my maternal grandparents were, in fact, agnostic. Of course, my father didn't believe in God at all, making him, technically, an atheist, but the differences in my parents' approach to religion had almost nothing to do with faith per se, and everything to do with a certain kind of orientation, a certain set of assumptions about one's conduct in the world, and the vocabulary that one chooses to frame and explain that conduct. In any event, my mother's family's God had long since detached Himself from Israel, becoming the God of good works and of giving to the Democratic party, which come to think of it is a better definition of God than some I've seen.

My parents were so dramatically mismatched that it's a wonder they ever so much as spoke more than two words to one another, let alone embarked on a marriage that lasted nearly five decades, growing stronger with age, and ending only with my mother's death. When I was a child, they basically didn't agree on anything, and in terms of Judaism per se, the hybrid of practice and belief they eventually came up with was so original that it practically constituted its own denomination. Except that it never worked, and kept shifting around, and was based on a half-dozen or so equally untenable and self-contradictory givens: first, that Dad's was the authentic voice of Judaism; second, that all of us were expected to practice Judaism the way Dad did, except that some of us couldn't, because we were too much like Mom—a principal that intersected and overlapped with the fact that none of us, including Mom (and except, maybe, David, who was my father's only son and therefore, from the paternal point of view, the carrier of the faith), could ever hope to attain Dad's level of observance and depth of commitment, so why bother? And finally, that there was a "right" way to do Judaism and a "wrong" way, and if you didn't do it the "right" way, you may as well not do it at all, except that to ignore the great grand moral vision and history of Judaism was to embark on a tragedy, a kind of spiritual suicide. Not that I understood, or ascertained, any of this when I was a child. But children do have a knack of apprehending things they cannot understand, and so each of us, in turn, apprehended, but didn't understand, the unspoken struggle between our parents over whose version of reality, whose way of perceiving of and operating in the world, would prevail. As for me, I was proud of being Jewish, but I also found the entire religion burdensome and overwhelming: something both slightly embarrassing and immensely daunting. It set me apart, inhabiting my genes and my synapses like some vague, unnamable, incurable virus.

Nevertheless, in some ways, life in McLean was idyllic, magical almost, and I was lost in its sheer natural beauty, in the streams that threaded their way through the woods near our house, the wildflowers that grew in great profusions of color along the sides of the roads, and the deep green gloom of the woods. I'd like to claim that I became so entranced by the natural world that, like the young Nabokov with his butterflies, I learned to identify certain classes of plants or animals or how to make bird calls, but I didn't: I merely wandered in it all, observing. As for my parents, they, too, were beautiful, and as glamorous as movie stars—he with his curly, prematurely silver hair and light green, penetrating eyes, she with her slim dark legs and Jackie Kennedy–style pink and yellow linen dresses, her black hair pulled back in a hair band, her black eyes sparkling. On the weekends, they played tennis with their friends and then sat on the patio, drinking Bloody Marys. In the winter, they skied or went to Bermuda, returning home with dark suntans and presents for us: beads, embroidered slippers, magically smooth, speckled shells mounted on small wooden platforms. And then on Friday nights, it all came crashing to a head, and we'd file into the dining room for Shabbat dinner. It was like living in a John Cheever novel edited by Isaac Bashevis Singer.

It was perfection, and I was in love with us, with the "we" of us, with my beautiful, high-spirited mother and her stories about climbing out the window of her dormitory room at Vassar after curfew; my father with his convertible Thunderbird that he drove too fast through the winding up-and-down roads in McLean; and even with our dog, George, who was so smart, we thought, that he was practically human, and in any case smarter than every other dog on the planet.

My own place in all this glory was somewhat tenuous, however. And that was because I took after, and looked like, my mother's side of the family, the Whitehills, none of whom were Moseses. In particular, I was said to resemble my mother's paternal grandmother, Grandma Etta. This wasn't good. Grandma Etta, who died before I was old enough to remember her, was a figure of fun, a model of what you weren't supposed to be: a kvetcher, a complainer, a nag, hypochondriac, and, worst of all, an obsessive worrier. My older sister, Binky, on the other hand, as well as my brother, were said to be solidly in the Moses camp, and therefore slated for dazzling and heady success. But me, with my Grandma Etta genes? To this day, I don't know if Grandma Etta deserved even half of her reputation; nor do I know what, if anything, she worried about.

My own worries revolved around issues of basic survival. For example, I worried about an invasion of Nazis, of whom, in point of fact, there weren't too many in McLean, Virginia, in the 1960s; I was also certain that the entire world would soon be incinerated by a nuclear bomb. At the age of twelve, I developed an ulcer. Unfortunately, my father didn't believe in sickness, so it was a while before my mother hauled me off to the pediatrician, who sent me home with a lifetime supply of Maalox and instructions to avoid fatty foods.

No matter: if I was a Whitehill, at least Mom had *someone* on her team. Unfortunately, I wasn't even very good at being a *Whitehill*. The Whitehills may have been "frivolous," but they were also gifted storytellers, loads of fun, spectacularly gorgeous, and great athletes—an entire race destined to be among the most popular kids in school—whereas I hovered perilously close to the bottom of the trough, just inches from plopping face-first into the sinkhole inhabited by social rejects and all-around retards who did spastic things with their faces. My one saving grace was that I liked to paint; at school, I hid in the sunny art room, lost in my paint brushes.

Years later, when I was living in New York and dating a very wealthy man whom my parents were crazy about and who even I assumed I was going to marry, my back went out. Specifically, it went out one morning when I bent down to retrieve a blouse from the floor. By the time I got to my job at *Mademoiselle* magazine, where I was an editorial assistant, I could barely move. I called my boyfriend, who diagnosed the problem as a muscle spasm and insisted that I get a cab and go to his place on the Upper East Side, where he could take care of me. His doctor put me on Valium and prescribed bed rest. And rest I did. For a full month, I did nothing but lie on my back in a complete stupor. At the end of the month, I still couldn't move. However, there had been *some* change: I had gone crazy. I felt like my entire being was about to explode, sending my brains and viscera, my bones and teeth, skittering and scattering along the highly polished parquet floors—an eventuality which at least would have relieved me of the awful feeling of being completely and flat-out nuts, proof of which was to be found in the fact that I was living with my boyfriend to begin with, when the fact of the matter was that I didn't even like him very much and could no more envision marrying him than I could envision joining the then-fledgling Taliban. Frankly, I preferred the company of my stuffed animals, Bumby (a rabbit) and Elephant.

I eventually wound my way to my first long-term psychoanalyst, to whom I explained that the basic and fundamental problem with me was actually, well, pretty straightforward: it wasn't that I was involved with a man whose tastes and inclinations were so far removed from my natural tendencies as to make him all but repugnant to me, or that, in addition, I had given this same man a kind of half-assed but nevertheless spoken promise to marry him, putting me in the position of living a complete and utter lie, but rather, that I was bad, always had been, and always would be. This was why my back had gone out, and this was also why I went around feeling like I had two heads, both of which were covered with oozing sores and other completely gross things that sprang from my overheated imagination. Moreover, I explained, this was nothing new, but rather, a discovery I had made as a very young child, though it was years before I had found the right verbal formula to describe my inner state. Now, however, it was so simple! And it was at the heart of everything, this badness of mine, and like gravity, it both pulled everything to it and explained the entire world. Not just my outer behavior, which was excessive and off-kilter, involving too much flirting and too many late nights, too much TV-watching and not enough jogging, but my very being, my very core, was bad. No wonder that every time I went to synagogue—usually with my parents and usually only because it was some major Jewish holiday or another and I was expected to, at the very least, show up—I felt like God was pissed off at me. I couldn't even read Hebrew, let alone read it with anything like the fluency of your average twelve-year-old bar or bat mitzvah student. I was so bad that they didn't have a name for it; so bad that I stood as an offense to everything good, wholesome, honest, and true. I was like an infection sent by an alien species. As a child, my badness leaked out of me in the way I crayoned, making a mess all over the page when everyone knows that you're supposed to stay inside the lines; and in the food that I constantly dribbled down the front of my shirt; and my piss-poor grades; and inability, far past the normal age for such things, to sleep without my stuffed bunny rabbit. Now it showed in my sex life, which was anything but salubrious, my constant, petty envy, and my ridiculous, boring job at *Mademoiselle,* where my duties mainly included things like typing up articles about finding your G-spot—a job which, incidentally, I wasn't even very good at, despite my belief that I was in fact smarter and certainly better-educated than most of my colleagues. (How could I not be? Even though I was cursed as a Whitehill, I was also a Moses.) It was in my eyes and my hair, my belly and my bottom, the soles of my feet and my fingertips. As a Jew, I was a total flop. Was it any wonder that, for as far back as I could remember, my father had been almost mortally disappointed in me?

Baton Rouge is a majority-black city of some 280,000 souls, of which a little more than one thousand are Jews. Between the roughly 220 Jewish families, there are two synagogues, both Reform. This didn't seem very promising to me, raised, as I had been, to think of the Reform movement as Judaism Lite, or, as I've since heard it put, "Christianity without Christ." Nor did there seem to be much likelihood that we'd ever feel like part of the Jewish community—these people who all sounded like Dolly Parton, wouldn't know a good bagel if you hit them over the head with it, and had never heard of Zabar's. Moreover, there was a decades-old feud going on between the more traditional of the two synagogues, Beth Shalom, and the less traditional, B'nai Israel. B'nai Israel adhered to the Classical Southern Reform style of worship—with an emphasis on the ethical laws as delivered by the Prophets and a de-emphasis on ritual and tradition— whereas Beth Shalom, we were told, was practically Orthodox in its insistence in doing everything by the book. Within three days of our having moved South, we were variously informed that (a) though it was Reform in name, Beth Shalom was filled with Torah-thumping fundamentalist nuts, the kind of embarrassingly Jewish Jews who follow every last jiggle and wiggle of the law, who roll their eyes heavenward, saying and doing embarrassing and awkward things that make you want to run screaming into the bushes; while (b) at B'nai Israel, they celebrated Hanukkah by erecting a Hanukkah bush, no one knew a lick of Hebrew, the autumn festival of Sukkot was observed by hanging Christmas ornaments on an indoor succah constructed out of metal wires (whereas the point of a succah, or booth, is that it's made outdoors, in the fields), and, most damning of all, attending worship services there was like going to group therapy. The two rabbis, we were told, hated each other. The "old" Baton Rouge Jews looked down their noses at the upstart Jews who hailed from north of the Mason-Dixon line and therefore had terrible manners and knew squat about anything of any importance at all, and the transplants considered the natives to be unsophisticated, parochial, self-hating, and willfully naive. The whole deal reminded me of the old joke about the Jewish man who, after living alone on a desert island for years and years, is finally rescued. Once ashore, his rescuers discover that the Jewish man, during his island exile, managed to build three separate buildings. The first, the man explains, is his house. The other two are the two synagogues in town. "Two synagogues?" his rescuers ask. "Why would you need two synagogues?" "This one here is the one I belong to," the man, gesturing, explains, "and this other one over there—that's the one I wouldn't be caught dead in."

Even before we'd moved, though, the Jewish community had somehow found out about us and made overtures, with both rabbis telephoning us in Washington to tell us that they were looking forward to our arrival, and to please not hesitate to call if there was anything they could do for us. (This was very different from Washington, D.C., where you'd have to die an agonizing death on the front steps of a synagogue for someone to so much as notice you.) The bidding war continued after our move, with invitations to peoples' homes, dinners out, homemade challah delivered to our doorstep, and more telephone calls. People were so nice I couldn't believe it. But they were also—how can I put it?—from another planet. At one of these dinners, people sat around talking about how to handle black help (one woman told me, "I told my girl that if I ever caught her so much as handling the silver, she'd be out on her ass") and later gathered around the piano, for a sing-along, which struck me as being so impossibly goody-goody that all I could do was sit on the sofa, in utter shock, trying not to look like I was suffering from post-traumatic stress disorder.

Of course, we could have said the hell with it and chucked the whole damn thing. What use was Judaism anyway? I mean, other than getting whole generations of its adherents slaughtered? (A juvenile joke that my son Sam recently told me goes like this: Q. What did the Nazi say to the black Jew? A. Go to the back of the gas chamber.) It certainly would have been easier to ignore it—simply and pleasantly melding into the larger surrounding population, eating crawfish at crawfish boils, and skipping out on torturously long worship services and the age-old anxieties about anti-Semitism, Israel, and the plight of the Jewish people. And what, after all, is *wrong* with being a nonbelieving, nonobserving ethnic but ethical Jew, a Jew who follows the moral teachings of the Bible, understands the various permutations of the verb *to schlep,* but disdains the rigors of keeping a kosher home and fasting on Yom Kippur? Most of my very own family fell into exactly this prototype, voting, acting, and thinking Jewish, without actually doing the religious part of it. But I had made the mistake, from the time I was a little girl, of wanting to know God. Worse, I cared, deeply, about my father, and his father before him, and so forth, all the way back to the founding family of my father's line—Michael Simon Levy and his wife, Betsy Levy, whose visages, captured in darkly elegant tones of black, brown, and cream, stared out from gilt frames on my grandparents' living room wall in Baltimore. (Michael Simon Levy was a rags-to-riches story, a tailor by trade who'd emigrated from Manchester, England, to the port of Baltimore just before the Civil War and within a decade or two founded a hat factory that in its day was the largest manufacturer of men's straw hats in the world.) How would *he* feel if not a single one of his great-great-great grandchildren adhered to the religion that had defined the very core of his being? How would my father, who still worshipped at his Orthodox synagogue in Georgetown and talked in reverent tones about his father, feel if not a single one of his children cared enough about Judaism to pass it on to the next generation?

Judaism, for me, was like finding a musty old box up in the attic and discovering that it was filled with family heirlooms. *You mean that stuff was up there all the time?* But for years—for years and years—I was such a wreck that all I wanted to do with it was shove it back into my father's face, to tell him to take the whole messy package and dump it in the nearest waste bin. I'd lie on the brown analytic sofa in my psychiatrist's office on East 78th Street, crying buckets over my distant, difficult father—planning my revenge, envisioning the day I'd finally be free of him and his whole oppressive, atavistic regime. And on and on I went, filled with such hatred for my father that it could only have been love, and, in the end, rather than throwing my father's religion aside, I began to study it. I studied and studied and studied, a kind of push-me-pull-you situation where half the time I was so bored and so uncomprehending—as in *I don't get it*—that it felt like my head was about to explode, like I was the one kid in a class full of twelve-year-olds who couldn't manage to conjugate simple French verbs. But I kept at it anyway, secretly yearning for a state of grace wherein I might set foot in a synagogue and simply feel that I belonged.

There's a beautiful passage in Lis Harris's *Holy Days,* a book I read shortly after my back recovered enough to allow me to get out of bed, in which the author recounts visiting a mikvah, or ritual bath, in Brooklyn. The book tells the story of a nonreligious woman who marries into a Hasidic family in Brooklyn, and how her entire life becomes defined by religion. (*Hasid* means "pious," and the *Hasidim* are adherents of the eighteenth-century teachings of the Ba'al Shem Tov, who taught a passionate, almost inflamed, Orthodox practice, in which love of God is paramount and the Word of God is alive, incandescent, and mysterious.) In accordance with the commandment to do so, Hasidic women purify themselves after their menstrual periods by immersing themselves in a mikvah. In the book's last scene, the author describes a sense of almost unworldly serenity that comes over her as she descends into the waters. When I finished the book, I burst into tears and vowed that the very next day I'd cross the bridge into Brooklyn and find a rebbe who might take me in and tutor me in the ways of the holy. But who was I kidding? Even as I envisioned my new, radiant, pure path, I knew that I'd no sooner devote myself to a life of Torah and kosher chicken soup than I'd grow wings and fly to Mars. I didn't *want* to give up the life I was living. I liked my tiny, narrow, fifth-floor walk-up on Avenue A, with its view, on one side, of the airshaft, and, on the other, of the crack-house across the street. I liked going shopping, and to the movies, and on dates. True, my love life was a joke, but I intended to fall in love, eventually, and for keeps—I just hadn't yet figured out how this was done. And most of all, I was going to be damned if I'd let someone else proscribe my life or tell me what to do. Also, there was this: Judaism, it seemed to me, was ambivalent, at best, on the subject of creativity. You couldn't make graven images; ergo, for centuries Jews didn't depict human beings at all. You couldn't gossip: indeed, the rabbis teach that once a tale has flown out of your mouth, it's scattered to the four winds like feathers from a feather pillow, impossible to retrieve; in the *Mishna Torah,* the Rambam elaborates on this theme, saying of the talebearer: "Such a person destroys the world." What, then, about writing? It always seemed to me that good writing is just a step or two away from really good gossip. True, some of my favorite writers—Saul Bellow, Philip Roth, Mordecai Richler—were Jewish, but not of the shul-going, kippah-wearing, tefillin-laying variety. But I would have sold my soul to the Devil, or even to the Republican Party, if it meant I could write like Saul Bellow or Philip Roth, and the hell with the Rambam and all his fervent, legalistic, hair-splitting, logic-torturing Judaism.

So I never crossed the bridge in search of enlightenment. I did, however, attend a Hasidic wedding right smack in the center of Brooklyn's Hasidic community. I'd been invited as the date of my rich boyfriend, the same man to whom I'd become semi-engaged even though he and I had nothing to say to one another and barely got along. This happened because his father, a businessman, met weekly with a Hasidic rebbe to study Talmud. When the rebbe's daughter got married, in Boro Park, my boyfriend's whole family was invited and, as I said, I tagged along.

I didn't know how to dress and ended up wearing the most conservative dress I had at the time—this tight-fitting, bright blue woolen number that fell just below my knees and hugged my butt, and which I liked wearing with my high-heeled lace-up black leather boots, a silk scarf, and big loopy gold earrings. I looked great. Still, I probably would have done better to borrow a neighbor's maternity clothes, or, for that matter, a tent. All the other women at the wedding were dressed in high Hasidic style: long sleeves, long skirts, conservative pumps, heavy makeup, and, if they were married, wigs (the idea being that a woman's real hair is too provocative to show to anyone other than one's husband). The bride, who looked to be about seventeen, was as pale as the moon and so tiny, in her white dress, that it was as if she were playing dress-up; the bridegroom, who couldn't have been much older, had the barest wisp of a beard and his skin was a waxy whitish-green. Both of them looked like they were about to faint. Who could blame them? After all, they'd only met two or three times previously. But, as I was told later, it wasn't fear that produced their waxen appearances, but hunger. In preparation for their marriage, both bride and groom had been fasting since the previous sundown.

Around and around the bride went, seven times around her groom, as the rabbi intoned the seven bridal benedictions. The blessing over the wine. The prayer for Zion's joy. In praise of Creation. For the joy of the bridal couple. The ketubah (wedding contract) was read. And finally, there was the exchange of rings. *Behold you are consecrated to me with this ring as my wife according to the law of Moses and the People Israel.* And then it was over. The marital couple exchanged a glance. The mother of the bride smiled. Bride and groom were led to a private room in order to break their fast. The festivities began.

Men on one side of the room, women on the other, with a cloth barrier down the middle. It was like the wedding scene from *Fiddler on the Roof,* minus the pogrom, and also minus the revolutionary boy-girl dancing. These late-twentieth-century Jews were far more reverent than Tevye's crowd and stayed on their side of the gender barrier as if forced by riot police. The women with whom I was seated seemed to feel sorry for me when they learned that, though I was already twenty-five, I was neither engaged nor married. Most of them were around my age or younger; all of them had children; many were pregnant. They talked about pregnancy and toilet-training and recipes, and though they tried to include me in the conversation, both they and I knew it was hopeless, and eventually they left me alone to smile vacantly at nothing.

My boyfriend, however, had a marvelous time. Over the cloth barrier that separated the men's from the women's side of the room, I saw him dancing ecstatically with the other men, his face flushed, his eyes gleaming, sweat damping down his hair. At one point, he danced so hard that his eyeglasses were knocked askew. I don't think I'd ever seen him look so happy.

"So?" he asked, later, as the two of us were whizzing back over the Manhattan Bridge in the back of a taxi. "What'd you think?"

"I think I'm glad I'm not a Hasidic Jew," I said. But I was lying. Despite my fierce commitment to choosing my own path, I would have loved to be a Hasidic Jew, to dance, inflamed, with the love of God. I would have loved to feel so close to Him that every pore cried out His name. I just didn't know how. I didn't have a clue.

Stuart and I ended up joining Beth Shalom synagogue, the "new" Baton Rouge synagogue, which had been founded in 1948—shortly after Israel was recognized by the United Nations—by a group of mainly northern-born Jews who couldn't go along with the philosophy then prevailing in the Classical Reform movement that declared that the age-old hope of a return to Zion was no longer part of the People Israel's quest. We joined Beth Shalom mainly because it was the more traditional of the two synagogues, and therefore closer to what both Stuart and I were accustomed to, and also because we liked the rabbi, who was then Paul Caplan. Actually, we loved Paul. He was tall and funny and warm and good-looking; he had a habit of making bad jokes; and he tended to be covered in small children. It sounds so dumb, but the fact that Rabbi Paul seemed to like me back was revelatory. I felt so comfortable with Paul that just about the first thing I told him was that I found much of Judaism off-putting and even cold. I then went on to say that I'd always had trouble with notions of the divine, that my Jewish education was haphazard, at best, and that more than once I'd wondered why I bothered being Jewish at all, given what a total pain in the ass it was. Eventually, I told him the whole long story of my mother— her struggle with cancer, her conviction that she was dying, her worries, and how, throughout her journeys through the oncology wards, I had remained aloof, as if she weren't my mother but someone else's entirely. Then I launched into my father. Paul pointed out that there was a reason the Torah doesn't command us to love our parents but, rather, to honor them. I found this biblical reassurance so liberating that I actually felt lighter, as if I were filled with fizzy bubbles and might float away.

Over the months, I found myself returning repeatedly to Paul's office at Beth Shalom, where I gave him a fairly detailed portrait of the holes in my education: I was woefully incapable of reading even the most basic Hebrew prayers, having long since made a habit of mumbling the liturgy along with the rest of the congregation, faking it in the hopes that no one would notice; more often than not I found services almost as boring, almost as alienating, as I had as a kid; I still didn't know why certain people were called up to pronounce a blessing over the Torah and couldn't keep the divisions of the holy books straight, let alone remember when the various components of the Talmud had been composed. And why was it that reading the great Jewish mystical texts, even in translation, felt like reading Sanskrit? "Have you ever thought about becoming an adult bat mitzvah?" Paul said. "No," I said. "Maybe you should," he said. Me? An adult bat mitzvah? That was a good one. The very idea of getting up in front of the congregation to chant Torah made me feel like I had sand in my lungs.

And anyway, I'd had my chance. My father may have attended Orthodox shul, a place where women didn't exactly rate, his entire adult life, but that hadn't stopped him from encouraging me, and both my sisters, to become b'nai mitzvah. I flat-out refused. Neither of my sisters became a bat mitzvah either, but my brother, David, had no such choice. As the only son of an only son (my father was, in fact, the sole male of his entire generation), the weight of the entire four-thousand-year-old Jewish tradition rested on his adolescent shoulders. He became a bar mitzvah at Congregation Tifereth Israel in Washington, D.C., in the fall of 1973. To this day, I remember sitting in the first row of the synagogue, vastly relieved that it was my brother, and not I, who had been forced to ascend the bimah at the front of the congregation and read from the massive Torah scroll.

"So?" Rabbi Paul said. "What about it?"

The Shema is the central statement of faith in Judaism. It's recited in every prayer service, in every synagogue in the world: *Shema Yisrael: Adonai Elohanu; Adonai echad.* (Hear, O Israel: The Lord is God; The Lord is One—or as a New Age rabbi I once heard put it: Listen up, oh you children of Israel! God and God alone is God—not power, not money, not ambition, not wealth—and God is at One and is One with the Whole Universe.) It's the prayer that was on the lips of the martyrs as they were led to the ovens at Auschwitz and the stakes of the Spanish Inquisition. As recorded in the book of Deuteronomy, it was given to Moses thirty-five hundred years ago and has been recited by Jews twice a day, in all places, at all times, continuously. The sages Hillel and Shammai, who lived around the time of the destruction of the Second Temple, debated what time the Shema should be recited, which we know about because their debates are recorded in the Talmud, or oral law—that marvelous, continuously cross-referenced record of rabbinical inquiry that was finally completed in written form in the fifth century. The Shema is said by some to be the "Jewish Pledge of Allegiance" and by others to be akin to a commandment to study. Try listening to it recited in a deep Southern accent. It just didn't sound *Jewish*. I felt so alienated from the Southern culture that I'd landed in—with its barbecues and crawfish boils, football frenzy and Wal-Marts, mega-churches and multiplexes—that I started writing short stories in the voice of a pregnant, black teenage illiterate girl. I showed a couple of them to my older sister, Binky, and after she read them, she said, "Who do you think you're kidding?" But I hadn't forgotten that I was white, married, secure, Jewish, and almost ridiculously privileged. I just didn't feel that way.

Before we moved to Baton Rouge, I'd freelanced fairly regularly for the *Washington Post* and gradually built up enough momentum to have something of a following. Largely because of the prestige of the *Post* on the one hand, and my own fragile, grasping, wounded ego on the other, this gave me no end of pleasure, particularly since, in Washington, you are what you do, and staying home and changing diapers—my primary occupation—just didn't cut the mustard. Whenever, at parties, I revealed that I was a mommy, there'd be this polite little silence, until my interlocutor excused him or herself, in search of more scintillating company. More often than not I'd be left by the hors d'oeuvres, holding my glass of white wine until I could feel crow's feet growing at the corners of my eyes. But then things started happening for me at the *Post,* and people started talking to me at parties. I figured that now that I was in Baton Rouge, the thing to do would be to go the next step—not just write articles, but write a whole book; not just write a book, but write a book that would land me on the best-seller list and the talk-show circuit—from whence I'd go soaring over the heads of everyone who had ever tormented me, with a giant sign that said, I TOLD YOU SO.

Not surprisingly, it didn't take long for the folks at Beth Shalom to notice that they had a writer in their midst. One day the copresident of the synagogue sisterhood called me to say that, since I was a writer, perhaps I'd like to contribute to the synagogue newsletter, which, she explained, might be an ideal place for me to break in professionally in Baton Rouge. I thanked her and hung up. I was a serious writer. I had my very own agent. And she was in *New York*. When my husband came home that night, I told him about how at last I'd really hit the big time courtesy of the Beth Shalom Synagogue newsletter, but he told me to forget about it, the sisterhood copresident was only trying to be nice. Then the *other* sisterhood copresident, Bev, was diagnosed with pancreatic cancer, and a friend of hers asked me if I'd like to write a kind of journal of her dying. The idea would be that through Bev's journal, the congregation would be kept informed of her journey, and Bev would be comforted by knowing that she wasn't alone in her plight. The journal was to be published in installments in the synagogue newsletter.

Bev was a large, friendly woman with dark, round eyes and a heavy manner who always appeared to give off an aura of dampness. She'd grown up in Baton Rouge and had a difficult marriage, which had resulted in two small children, one a newborn; she'd had some previous trouble in her love life, too, which had produced an earlier child, a boy with whom Sam sometimes played. She struck me as being the ultimate small-town girl, so small-town that she didn't even know that she was small-town. She didn't seem to have a clue that, beyond Interstate 10, another world existed, or that others might come from that world. Nor did she seem interested in ideas, or the life of the mind, or imagination, or dreams. Rather, she struck me as being rooted to the earth, like a farm animal. I didn't dislike her, but I didn't like her, either. But something about her plight drew me in. She was only three or four years older than I was.

I began to visit Bev's bedside regularly, first at her small, brick home in the outer limits of Baton Rouge, and then in the hospital. She was sometimes zonked out on painkillers and sometimes wild with anger. In either case, she was more concerned with everyday things than with anything even remotely related to the big questions. There was no "What happens to me afterward?" Or "Has my life been meaningful?" Or even "Why me?" I thought this was absolutely amazing. Once she got into a loud fight with her mother over the issue of her children's school lunches. Her mother argued that premade Lunchables from the supermarket were sufficient, while Bev insisted that it was both more nutritious and cheaper to make a sandwich and throw it in a brown paper bag. Another time, she railed against her husband, who she claimed was dealing with her imminent death by spending all his time at the gym. She talked about how much she missed food, which she could no longer eat, and how much she'd liked certain movies. Every time I went to visit her, I wrote up a little journal entry for the synagogue newsletter. After six months of ineffective treatment and countless hospital stays, Bev was allowed to go home, where her sisters, both nurses, cared for her. One sister later told me that, in the instant before she died, Bev opened her eyes and said, "Enough."

After she died, every single member of Bev's family called to thank me for writing about her. Then, in February, the sisterhood dedicated its annual Shabbat service to her, and asked me to speak. I ascended the bimah, and, my voice shaking—from nervousness more than anything—I talked about how I'd gotten to know Bev at her sickbed, and how she'd allowed me to witness her progression toward death. And in this way I finally became a part of the synagogue community. The months passed. My mother was feeling better. We'd been in Baton Rouge a full year.

Soon after he'd started second grade, Sam came home and announced that his friend David's father had died of cancer, leaving a wife, Susan, as well as David and another child, and giving me such a severe case of hypochondria that for weeks afterward, I went around poking myself in the groin and armpits, in search of tumors.

For crying out loud, I thought. Did anyone *not* have cancer?

Susan was one of those private-school moms who seem to have nothing better to do than drive me crazy with endless requests for brownies. And if it wasn't brownies, it was that I show up to go on a field trip to the Children's Museum. And if it wasn't chaperoning, it was organizing a tea for the lower-school teachers. Didn't she know that I was way too busy with important things to do that mommy shit? It was weird, too, because Susan, unlike almost every other parent at the school, was black: meaning that, according to my preferred stereotypes, she was supposed to be at least a *little bit* hip. Despite her hyper-momness, I'd always liked Susan—it was hard not to—and, more to the point, in Judaism, attending to the bereaved isn't optional.

The funeral was held in a big box of a place constructed of sheet metal, like an airplane hangar. It was an old-fashioned, black, gospel-style service, with a lot of singing, several eulogies, and more singing. Overhead, ceiling fans whirred. At last it seemed that the whole thing was beginning to wrap up. But then, from her place in the first pew, a slender woman with coffee-brown skin, wearing a red dress and red high-heeled shoes, stood up and began to dance, her arms waving toward the heavens, her face upturned. Every part of her body was in motion, as if she were animated by pure spirit. Then she began to moan, the moan rising to a kind of keening, or wailing, only it wasn't mournful, or violent, but rather, happy, almost joyous. Who was she? I couldn't for the life of me recognize her, and I leaned over to ask Stuart. The dancer, he said, was Susan.

Since then I've attended more funerals than I can count, most of them for victims of AIDS, and many of them in black evangelical churches. The minute people start singing, particularly if it's a really good gospel number—and what gospel number *isn't* a really good gospel number?—I begin to bawl. I find these services so moving that my tears, as often as not, are an expression of gratitude as much as of loss. But to this day I've never witnessed anything like the disturbing, mysterious, inspirational sight of Susan, her bright red dress like a flame, dancing.

I, too, wanted to be a bright red flame, dancing. I, too, wanted to be filled with a faith so buoyant that it could carry me beyond myself, beyond sorrow, beyond memory even, and right smack into the embrace of eternity.

Torah and Torah study are at the very center of Jewish religious life. Thus, portions of it are read aloud in the synagogue throughout the year, in a regular cycle, until the entirety of the Torah has been completed. On the holiday of Simchat Torah, you finish reading the last few verses of

Deuteronomy and immediately start all over again, with the first verses of Genesis. Rabbi Joseph Telushkin puts it this way: "Because the Torah is the only document that the Jewish tradition regarded as containing God's words and only God's words, it is considered to be the holiest object in Jewish life . . . in effect, the constitution of the Jewish people." A beautiful idea, even if it was, for me, tough to swallow. Even so, shortly after Susan's husband was laid to rest, when Simchat Torah rolled around, I thought that maybe it would be a good idea to attend the celebration, if only to take advantage of the kosher nosh that was sure to be spread out on paper doily-covered trays in the synagogue's social hall. I'd actually never been to Simchat Torah services before, and didn't know what to expect, but when we got to synagogue, it was just the same-old same-old. Rabbi Paul ascended the bimah, told us what page to turn to, and started. How cut-and-dried, how rote, the whole thing seemed. I was standing up, I was sitting down, standing up, sitting down—Jewish aerobics. I was desperate to be home, curled up in bed with a novel. Why hadn't I been born an evangelical Christian? At the very least, I would have been permitted to eat bacon.

A million years later, when services were finally over, Sam butted his head into my stomach, and, having secured my attention, said: "Get *up*, Mom, don't you want to dance?" Dance? No, I didn't want to dance. But the thing is, it was Simchat Torah, and on Simchat Torah you're supposed to dance. Think of Chagall with his bearded, black-clad Old World Jews embracing the Torah scrolls in midair. Not that I felt like a person in a Chagall painting. I got up and performed a sorry excuse for a dance, anyway. Boy, did I feel dumb. "What's your problem, Mom?" Sam said. "Why aren't you dancing?"

"Go away," I said.

"But you love to dance, Mom," Sam said, which was true. Ever since I was a little girl, following my mother around the house to the sounds of Zero Mostel singing "If I Were a Rich Man," I'd loved nothing better than shaking my groove-thing, preferably to just about anything by the Rolling Stones, though I also liked all kinds of other bands, none of which, however, sang in biblical Hebrew.

Rabbi Paul appeared before me, a Torah scroll in his arms. "Have you had a turn?" he asked.

Had I had a turn? No, I hadn't, and Rabbi Paul, of all people, knew it. After all, I was still trailing all my unresolved conflicts, my bag of ancient bloodied psychic rags, my resentment, my bitterness, my cynicism, my doubts. I'd never donned a tallit, never been called for an aliyah, never become a bat mitzvah. My Hebrew wasn't worth a damn. So no: I hadn't had a turn; indeed, I'd never felt that the Torah—and everything that Torah represents, which is no more than the combined wisdom and teaching of four thousand years of Jewish thinking, plus the daughter religions it spawned—was really mine to hold at all. What gave me the right to dance with the Torah?

"Here," Rabbi Paul said.

The Torah was in my arms. I felt weird. Plus that sucker—yards and yards of pure parchment held together on wooden spindles and adorned with silver crowns—was *heavy*. By now, too, we had moved from the air-conditioned sanctuary outside to the front lawn. Here we were, this little circle of Jews on the grass, doing this little circle dance. "Dance, Mommy, dance," my children said, and as the traffic whizzed by on the old Thomas Jefferson Highway, the massive edifice of the Jefferson Baptist Church looked on from the adjoining lot, and the mosquitoes buzzed around our heads, I danced with the Torah in my arms.

3

Dr. God

Philomena was the most alone person I have ever known. She'd lie in her bed at St. Anthony's—in the same corner room that had once belonged to Little Chuck—and cry. Every now and again, she'd take out the engagement ring that her former fiancé had given to her before she'd gotten sick, before she blew up like a blowfish, her cheeks massive, her forehead shiny, before her legs began to give out on her and she could no longer control her bladder, before she started wearing giant-sized Pampers and regurgitating even small amounts of orange juice. She'd hold the ring in her hands, turn it over, put it back in a small black box, and place the box in her top dresser drawer, with her socks and underpants. "Why don't you wear it on a chain around your neck?" Caroline, one of the caregivers, would ask her. "It will remind you that you are loved."

"This I cannot do."

Philomena was Nigerian: this part of her history I knew. The rest was fuzzy. More than once, she'd told me her story, but the pieces didn't add up. For example, she told me that she'd contracted HIV from an accident that had occurred to her while she was at work, as a physical therapist somewhere in Florida. She said that one day when she was working in a hospital, she slipped and fell on the floor, where she came into contact with contaminated blood. This made no sense to me. I also couldn't figure out how she had gotten from Nigeria to Florida, or why, after Florida, she'd come to Baton Rouge. All I knew was that every Tuesday morning when I showed up at St. Anthony's, she was in her room, waiting.

Sometimes she'd just lie there, utterly silent, but other times, she couldn't shut up. "Please, Jennifer, to take me on a drive. They do not like me here. They want me gone. Take me away from here where they do not take proper care of me. I have a university diploma. This they do not understand. I am from Africa. They do not understand Africa. They think it is all darkness there, but it is all darkness here, all darkness, and without light. I have such a terrible pain. I cannot eat. I cannot drink. They make me take food, but I cannot eat it. Why do they force me to take food, which I can no longer keep down?"

"Philomena, now, you's wearing that Pampers I helps put on you, right?"

"You see what I mean, Jennifer? They treat me as if I were an infant, an ignorant worker, a person without an education. I have a university degree. I am an educated person."

"Now, Philomena, you know that ain't the way it is. We all love you here, but Jennifer can't take you out in her van if you going to have an accident."

"I am fine."

And so I'd take her out, driving up Government Street through midcity and into the Garden District, where my own airy home sits well back from the street behind two enormous magnolia trees—the lovely, leafy green Garden District, where people drink iced tea in deeply shaded back gardens, and wisteria vines cover brick walls—and onto the city lakes, where I'd drive slowly, chattering away about nothing in particular, and Philomena, by my side, would gaze out, the tears sliding slowly down her brown cheeks.

On other days, I'd point my minivan in another direction, heading to a nearby subdivision of enormous one- and two-story houses sitting back on perfectly manicured broad green lawns: we'd pass French chateaus, neo-Tudors, Greek Revival monstrosities, and enormous raised Acadian cottages with six-car garages. The streets were always silent: it's a neighborhood of houses seemingly devoid of human occupants, but it's the closest thing Baton Rouge has to Beverly Hills or Lakeshore Drive. How some people live, huh? I'd say, as if I'd never been in this corner of Baton Rouge before, as if my children didn't play with the children of these sprawling Prairie-style mansions, swimming in their backyard swimming pools and watching their giant-screened televisions. I'd be so full of shit that I'd embarrass myself, but Philomena, gazing out the window, never seemed to notice.

What is it about Philomena that got to me? No one else could much stand her. Even the caregivers had a hard time with her. Even Caroline, who is so kind that, more often than not, I had to fight the urge to crawl into her lap. But Philomena was adamant in her obstinacy, fierce in her right to misery. There were days when she wouldn't so much as pretend to try to help herself, refusing to stand on her own legs, insisting that she was too weak, too sick, that she needed to be carried. Other days she did nothing but cry.

The thing is, at St. Anthony's, no one cries. It just doesn't happen. I don't know why, exactly, though I suspect that, for the majority of the residents, tears are a luxury they haven't allowed themselves since childhood. Sure, there are the occasional sniffles, but real tears—tears of grief or rage, fear or exaltation—never.

God alone knows what the folks at St. Anthony's would think of me if they knew that not only do I cry buckets at the drop of a hat, but also that I actually pay money to someone to listen to me while I cry. God knows what they'd think of me if they knew that I—with my big house and healthy children, my summers in Maine and book-lined rooms—still feel so alone and so bereft that at times I feel as if my heart has been removed from me or that all my blood has been drained.

When I was seventeen and a senior in high school, I went to a party, where I got stoned out of my mind on hash and immediately slid into a pit of paranoia and misery so deep that I thought my brain would melt. By the time I got home—not that I remember how I had accomplished this—I was even worse. I had long since given up praying, but now, as I splashed my face and hands in cold water in a useless attempt to restore my perceptions to something approaching sanity, I realized that I was in deep shit for sure and didn't have a choice. I fell to my knees on the bathroom mat and muttered a couple of phrases of Hebrew, followed by some more in English. My thoughts flew like bats, squawking. "Please help me," I pleaded. Nothing happened. Then it occurred to me that I was praying to the wrong guy. It was 1977, a time when Jesus was making the rounds at Langley High School in a fairly big way, so much so that a fair number of people whom I counted among my friends had joined the high school Christian club, Young Life, meeting after school to sing folk songs, hold hands, and talk. It was unspeakably cheerful—like some icky combination of the Girl Scouts, Miss America, and Big Bird—but I was secretly envious of the Young Lifers, who all seemed to walk around with this hazy cloud of sweetness hovering about them, as if they *were* on drugs, which they weren't. So I knew all the nice things that Jesus could do for you, if only you asked in the right way. Still on my hands and knees in the bathroom, I once again begged God to help me out, and then, when He didn't, I announced to Him that I just couldn't take any more of this crap, and was therefore going to take my problems to His only begotten son. "Okay, Jesus," I said out loud, and then I explained that I was willing to be a traitor, not only to my family but also to the countless martyrs who had died because they were Jewish, and make a deal: I'd abandon my own tradition and embrace Jesus instead—provided that he pull me out of the state of extreme terror I was in, courtesy of the big, orange, plastic bong that someone had thrust toward me at the party I'd attended earlier that night. (What had I been doing at that party, anyhow? I hated parties, was terrified of boys, and always ended up alone, leaning against a wall, trying to look like I didn't care that no one was interested in talking to me.) "Please, Jesus," I said over and over. "I'll accept you as my personal savior. I mean it." Nothing happened. I stood up, washed my face again, and stared at my reflection in the mirror, trying to will back some perception of myself as a human being rather than an *animal* creature, some humanoid with weirdly yellowed eyeballs and fuzz growing on top of her head. Okay, Jesus, I'm *waiting*. Just say the word, and I'll switch allegiances. Come into my heart. I'll believe. I'll have faith. I'll sing your praises. *Really.* But Jesus didn't answer me, so I left the bathroom and went to get my mother instead. She padded out of her room in her nightgown and sat by the side of my bed while I talked and talked and talked—a flurry of words and jumble of confusion—until I had exhausted myself and fell into a deep sleep. And in the morning, I woke up to discover that I was still a failed Jew.

Now I realize that perhaps God answered me after all, and moreover, He answered me in a way that wouldn't send me into the psych ward— which an appearance from Jesus surely would have accomplished pretty swiftly. He sent Mom, and Mom had had enough. She hauled me off to an old-fashioned Freudian psychoanalyst with startlingly bright blue eyes, a powerfully soothing voice, antiquated convictions regarding women, and an office filled with line drawings. And it was here, in his hushed office in Northwest Washington, overlooking a small green space with perfectly manicured grass, that I got my first taste of liberation. Dr. Berman put me on antidepressants and speculated that in all likelihood I'd been displaced, in the affections of my father, by my brother. He interpreted my dreams and handed me boxes of tissue. He told me that there was happiness in my future in the form of marriage and children. I loved every minute of it. It was my little secret—these wonderful, protracted crying sessions of mine, this wonderful, wise old man who would cure my soul. I went to Dr. Berman three times a week after school, driving myself through McLean and across the river in the light blue, secondhand VW bug that my parents had bought for Binky during her last year of high school, sneaking off, stealthily, like someone embarking on an affair. I had to be very quiet about Dr. Berman, because, in those days, in Washington, no one went into therapy. Or at least no one talked about it. Moreover, no one in my extended family of cousins, aunts and uncles, and second cousins—let alone my hard-driving, non-talking father—would so much as consider such a step. It just wasn't done. We were *German* Jews: we pulled ourselves up by our own damn bootstraps, thank you very much. We didn't whine or moan or complain, and we sure as hell didn't consult psychotherapists—a suspect species of overly sissified intellectuals whose dubious remedies were, like facelifts, for self-indulgent New Yorkers, movie stars, and spoilt housewives. But Dr. Berman patched me up sufficiently well to send me off to college, in Boston, where I immediately fell madly in love with a boy who recited poetry, taught me how to drive a stick shift, and took me out to lovely romantic bistros where we drank red wine and talked about literature, art, and music. (I had by then discovered books.) This beautiful, graceful, brilliant boy seemed to think that I was equally beautiful, graceful, and brilliant, and when I was with him, I felt as if I'd shed my old, ugly feathers and grown plumes. Unfortunately, during my second year of college, he dumped me for a girl he'd met in graduate school, thereby leaving me with such a strong sense of having been abandoned and rejected that, more than twenty years later, I found myself in Baton Rouge, in yet another psychiatrist's office, sobbing as if the whole episode had just happened. My new therapist, unlike all the previous ones, wasn't male, or Freudian, or Jewish, but female and strictly non-Freudian, both a German and a devout, practicing Catholic. In other words, she was of the people who had shoved my people into the ovens. I didn't have a whole lot of confidence that she'd be able to help me, but I was desperate.

By then psychiatry had become, for me, a kind of secular religion—a separate, parallel track—as I think it probably is for a lot of people. You no longer confess your sins; instead, you confess your story—your impressions, your weaknesses, your apprehensions, your fantasies. You talk about sex. In fact, you talk about everything but God, and you discover that the world isn't fallen, or incomplete, or unredeemed: it's just neurotic as hell. Evil people suffer from poor self-esteem; good people are self-confident, the recipients of good parenting. Most of the many therapists I've seen over the years (switching therapists every time my husband dragged me to a new city) viewed my yearning to connect with God as part and parcel of my ability to *project:* what I really wanted, they hinted, was to be taken care of by my *actual* father, the Washington lawyer with the curly, silver hair and pale green eyes, only this time on my own terms. After all, they pointed out, not only did I concoct people out of words every time I sat down to write, but also, I still clung to the belief that my stuffed animals had feelings and personalities of their own. Indeed I never did outgrow my stuffed rabbit, Bumby—something that my mother found more than a little puzzling—nor had I been able to give up my attachment to Elephant, who had accompanied me to college, moved with me, afterward, to New York, and soon thereafter started offering me advice on all kinds of subjects. (In fact, it was Elephant who first urged me to marry Stuart, pointing out that, unlike other men I'd taken up with, Stuart was someone whose company I actually enjoyed.) Wasn't it obvious, given my reflexive and unconscious knack for making people and creatures up, that my feelings of displacement from God were no more than an extension of my feelings of displacement from my mother and father? And wasn't all of religion, when you got down to brass tacks, no more than man's pathetic attempt to comfort himself in the face of overwhelming unknowns? Even the extremely talented and gentle psychoanalyst, whom I saw for almost four years in New York, himself a Jew, couldn't fathom why anyone would cling to religion; true to his principles, he practiced on Yom Kippur—the holiest of all holy days in the Jewish calendar—and if you chose to indulge in your atavistic tribal ritual and attend synagogue rather than show up for your appointment, well, that was just your tough luck. He'd still charge you. I loved him anyway. Ten years later, I named my first child, Samuel, after him. The name means "God has heard."

When my mother finally got well enough, after her initial bout with cancer and chemo, to travel again, she came to visit us in Baton Rouge, a place she'd never been before and could barely imagine. One day, as I was driving with her to pick Sam up from school, she looked out the window at the sagging shotguns, the skinny black kids playing on the uneven sidewalks, and the broken windows, and said: "I swear to God, Jennifer, I'd rather be dead than poor." And that had been just over Perkins Road, near my house in the Garden District, in an area of town known as "old South Baton Rouge," an old, proud neighborhood—or at least it had been proud, before crack cocaine came in and ruined everything, driving most of the older residents out, and abandoning the neighborhood to its current gap-toothed look, with some houses occupied and others left to rot. But at St. Anthony's, the feeling—at least among the people who worked there—was exactly the opposite. They looked around and saw all the misery that rich people inflicted on each other, all the alienation, all the fathers not talking to sons, and daughters moving away, and divorces, and squabbles over business deals gone south, and big houses filled to overflowing with all kinds of useless, expensive, pretentious junk, and alcoholism—grandparents in different parts of the country, cousins who hadn't been heard from in decades—and felt sorry for *us*. (Not that there isn't all kinds of the same misery going on among poor people, but it has a slightly different flavor.) One day when I was sitting with Philomena, Joanna popped her head into the room, sat herself down, and, apropos of nothing, said, "I ain't rich, Jennifer, but I am rich. I'm rich in Jesus. What more do I need?" From her bed, Philomena began to mutter, "Jesus, Jesus, Jesus." I looked at Philomena, and then at Joanna, and saw, as if for the first time, what had been before me ever since I'd first met her. The woman was so overflowing with the palpable love of God that you can could see it on her, like a glow; so overflowing that it poured out of her and into her surroundings and then into song: *He's an on-time God, yes, He is! Job said He may not come when you want Him, but He'll be here right on time, I say that he's an on-time God, yes, He is!*

Most nights, in the privacy of my bedroom, I fall on my face and pray. Even so, I don't have one-tenth the inner peace that Joanna has, not one-tenth the sense that God's handiwork is everywhere, within and without. (Dear God, let me know that You're near, let me see Your face, hear Your voice, Dear God, be with me; tell me what to do, and I will hasten to do it.) And so I write down my dreams and pray for inspiration, and once a week trundle myself off to a German Catholic psychotherapist, where I sit and talk about all my ancient wounds and cry buckets of tears.

But one day, as I was sitting in therapy sobbing about something or another, I discovered that my Baton Rouge therapist not only didn't condemn my religious impulses but actually encouraged me to talk to God on a daily basis, going so far as to urge me to ask God to allow me to feel His heavenly love. Therapy-wise, I got the picture, the idea being that if it wasn't always easy for me to feel my actual father's fatherly love, it would be good for me to get some paternal strokes from the Father of Us All. A conscientious student, I was very literal about my assignment. "Dear God above," I prayed, "if You can hear me, please let me feel Your fatherly love." The next day, a book on Jewish theology arrived in the mail from my father, who had inscribed it to me, in Hebrew. This is what Dad had written: *Im ahova, Abba.* With love, from Daddy. This totally blew me away. The next week, I asked Joanna if I might join her one day at church—which I did, driving for miles up past the airport to a rural area of East Baton Rouge Parish, where I found the little white clapboard church that Joanna belonged to, looking like something straight out of Grandma Moses, only minus the snow—and the week after that, I knocked on Rabbi Paul's office door at Beth Shalom and told him that I wanted to start studying for the bat mitzvah that I'd absolutely refused to have some thirty years earlier.

"Mazel tov," he said.

As AIDS started spreading out of the strictly gay population and into the general drug-abusing population, more and more women started moving in to St. Anthony's. There was Sarah, a former prostitute and inveterate liar, who one day wheedled me into taking her to a nearby food bank, where she stocked up on canned goods, even though—as I later learned—as a resident of St. Anthony's, she was no longer eligible for the food bank. There was Ursula, who had three young children and a fiancé serving time at Angola. Valerie was so huge, her body bloated by drugs, that she had to be lifted off her bed by means of a specially designed medical lift. The caregivers would put her in a lounge chair, brush her hair and her teeth, and wheel her into the front room, where she would nod in and out all day long, waking up only long enough to be fed. Her family had dumped her at St. Anthony's, and she was expected to live only a few months. All the old crew—the people who had been, for me, the first generation—were long gone.

Alone among the other residents, the ones who had lost their eyesight and the ones who had lost their ability to walk, the ones whose families had turned their backs on them and the ones who had committed terrible crimes, only Philomena cried. She cried and cried and cried, the tears falling down her face like a waterfall, a force of nature, a filmy curtain of grief.

Her family, in Nigeria, didn't even know that she was sick, let alone that she was sick with AIDS. They would be shunned, she said, if such news were known. She would bring shame on them. Their name would be dishonored.

"Why don't you write to them?" Caroline would say. "They your family, and they loves you. They would want to know it, if you're sick."

"No, I cannot," Philomena would answer in her precise, old-fashioned, African-inflected English. "I cannot do this. Soon I will die here. There is no more to be said."

One day Philomena asked me to read from a book that was lying on top of her dresser. It was one of those cheesy paperbacks with flimsy, oily-smelling pages that you sometimes see in remainder piles at libraries or stacked up at sidewalk sales. I can't remember the book's title, though I think it was something like *Finding Health through Jesus of Nazareth*. In any event, the premise of the book is that sickness is a physical manifestation of sin, which, happily, can be cured by faith. A pretty premise, except for one wrinkle: if your faith isn't strong enough, that's your tough luck. Cancer? Your fault. Multiple sclerosis? Ditto. But Philomena insisted that I read this pile of crap to her, so I pulled up a chair, opened the book, and began. I don't mind reading aloud, and always enjoyed reading to my children, but this stuff was rough going—the prose so garbled and thick-tongued that I had a hard time getting my mouth around it, and the message itself, the meaning under the heap of words, downright repulsive. After fifteen minutes or so, I said: "Philomena, you don't actually believe this, do you?" She looked at me with eyes made huge by thick glasses and cried.

And that's another thing about living here, in the Deep South, among the Christian faithful. Sometimes it's enough to make you forget about all the good ways that Christianity plays itself out in the world and downright hate Christianity as a whole—for its blind insistence on the simplest of simple roads, for its triumphalist views of right and wrong, for its selective and literal reading of the Hebrew Bible, moral superiority, and utter, non-sensical rigidity. Not to mention the tendency of some Christian denominations to side with the bad guys on just about every issue—desegregation (the Southern Baptists came out firmly against it), equal rights for women (ditto), gay rights (remember the boycott of Disney World?). And just because the Supreme Court has ruled conclusively, and more than once, that prayer at public schools is illegal, doesn't mean that you should stop doing it—after all, it's a Christian country, isn't it? Even the state law school, which happens to be my husband's employer, turns a blind eye to the niceties of the First Amendment's insistence on the separation of church and state and hangs an enormous Christmas wreath over its imposing neo-classical entrance every December. It sometimes seems that the almighty hand of God came along with a divine vacuum cleaner and suctioned every last brain cell out of every last brain in East Baton Rouge Parish. I have a neighbor—a devout Christian with whom I often stop to chat—who, every time she sees me, tells me that she loves the Jewish people, of whom she knows precisely one member. This is a woman who wouldn't hurt a hair on the head of any living creature, who is kind and generous, exuding warmth and acceptance, and yet she also theorizes that the reason Jews have suffered so much throughout our long history is because, as recounted in the Hebrew Bible, we are so stiff-necked. She cited the example of the Hebrews who, upon entering the Promised Land under the leadership of Joshua, didn't raze all the Canaanite cities and kill all their inhabitants, as instructed by God, but instead left some people living, taking them instead as booty. "Why didn't they do what God told them to do?" my neighbor said as the two of us chatted under the shade of an enormous live oak tree while above us birds twittered and frittered about, calling to each other from branch to branch. I mean, what do you do with people like that?

My father once offered this explanation of the Christian story to me. Based on his own extensive reading on the matter, he said that he was convinced that Jesus of Nazareth, an illiterate Jew, did indeed preach in the small towns in and around the Galilee, gathering a following along the way. Like many Jews at the time, his most fervent wish was to overthrow the brutal Roman occupation, and he believed he would do so, with the help of God, as predicted by the Hebrew prophets. A known anti-Roman provocateur, he entered Jerusalem on a donkey—again with an eye toward stagecraft, as the prophetic account places the future messiah-liberator of Judea on an ass—creating a buzz until the Romans found him and strung him up, along with the other fifty or one hundred thousand anti-Roman Palestinian Jews who had the temerity to fight the power. Only most people don't know about all those *other* anti-Roman Palestinian Jews who were tortured to death around the same time that Jesus of Nazareth was. (The account comes from the first-century Roman historian Tacitus.) They only know about Jesus.

But then what happened? How did an illiterate Jewish carpenter get promoted to God?

Dad said: "The Greco-Roman world was terribly corrupt and brutal. And Judaism was still tied to the land of Israel and the Temple rituals. But the new Jesus movement, with its accessibility to God and disdain of worldly power, appealed to the masses." What Dad didn't talk about was how, once Constantine made Christianity the official state religion in the year 312, the cross became the sword.

It's one of those tricky little questions that most Jews I know, myself included, try to avoid talking about in polite company, but the truth is that most Jews (or at least those, in my immediate family, whom I have polled on the subject) just don't *get* Christianity, viewing it as an ever-changing mishmash of conflicting stories, all of them resting on the head of this poor schmuck of a Jewish boy who was hideously tortured to death. And then that same Jewish boy—or rather, his teachings—are twisted and twisted beyond recognition, to be used as a justification to vilify and harm Jews, homosexuals, women, Muslims, or, depending on the century, all of the above. This is, as my mother would say, completely *meshugge*.

And yet at St. Anthony's, Jesus fills the rooms and hallways with hope; He comforts the sick; He refreshes the weary. He is everywhere. And this particular Jesus—the Jesus of love—occasionally comes into my heart, too, filling me with ecstasy and beckoning me to return to my best, my most essential, self. And the thing is, I like this Jesus just fine, not that I'd want to discuss my friendliness toward him with my rabbi. In fact, I'm just crazy about this Jesus, the Jesus-as-love Jesus, the one who comes into your innards and fills you with energy and openness and a kind of dazed amazement at the very fact that you're here, that you're alive, and that, what's more, you're *cognizant* of your own existence. In fact, that Jesus is so cool that, last time I checked, he was adamant that all three of my children become b'nai mitzvoth, that I go ahead and learn how to speak Hebrew, and that when I pray, I address no one other than Adonai, the *I-Am-Who-I-Am,* the *I-Was-I-Am-I-Will-Be* of Judaism. This Jesus? He's aces. I don't, however, much like the *Passion of the Christ* Mel Gibson–type Jesus, the one who says that all kinds of people, especially gays, Democrats, city-dwellers, intellectuals, and Jews, are, if not downright evil, then at least the enemies of all that is good. This latter Jesus—who needs him? He's done nothing but spill blood ever since his debut in Rome, on the arm of Constantine, some seventeen centuries ago.

Judaism began at Sinai and is based on covenant. To be Jewish is to agree to the terms of that covenant: to be Israel, God's beloved. Or as the Song of Songs puts it: "He brought me to His banquet room / And His banner of love was over me / Sustain me with raisin cakes / Refresh me with apples / for I am faint with love." Or later: "My beloved is mine / And I am His." The first-century Jewish sage Rabbi Akiva taught that the Song of Songs was "the Holy of Holies," and that "had the Torah not been given, the world could have been conducted according to the Song of

Songs." As the bride of God, Israel is redeemed. Read from this point of view, the entire Hebrew Bible is a love story between the people of Israel and God

"Jesus loves you, baby," Joanna or Caroline, or sometimes Martha or Miss Marie, says as I leave St. Anthony's, fumbling around in my Coach bag for my car keys, thinking of a certain tribal rug that I'd like to buy for my study or whether that small lump in my inner thigh is thigh cancer or just plain cellulite.

For a while, particularly when I first started volunteering at St. Anthony's, and would come home with all these stories about all these people dying peacefully in the arms of Jesus, my husband worried that I was about to cross over to the other side—that I was about to sign up on the Jesus team, as I had almost done twenty-five years earlier, in high school. But the deepest part of my deepest faith believes in the words of the Shema: Hear, O Israel, the Lord is God, the Lord is One!

And that's the little secret that they don't tell you in Sunday school: Jesus, Adonai, the Buddha, Yaweh, Allah, Krishna—they're all the same dude. Not that any of them could save Philomena.

4

Hebrew on the Bayou

After Bev died, I felt like I had turned a corner at the synagogue: now I was a part of the community. For better and for worse, there was no going back. I couldn't avoid the annoying old lady who cornered me after services to give me ideas for books she wanted me to write, such as the one about her really cute cat, any more than I could avoid my own face in the mirror. And what about the nutcase who was convinced that there was a left-wing conspiracy to bring bolshevism to the United States, railing on and on against the evils of feminism, secular humanism, and popular music? The woman who believed that the synagogue was socially divided between what she called the *haves* and the *have-nots,* insisting that I join her in a scheme to take over the synagogue board? The man who had never gotten over women reading from Torah (something that women within the Orthodox movement are still prohibited from doing) and was convinced that Judaism had gone to rack and ruin? The octogenarian who kept landing in the hospital with pulmonary problems? Actually, this particular octogenarian, Mr. Adams, pretty quickly endeared himself to us and therefore proceeded to wriggle his way into our lives and our affections. Stuart and I had made the mistake of visiting him in the hospital once, and ever since, we were on his call list, such that every couple of weeks or so he'd telephone to ask what the problem was—he hadn't seen us in a while, and when were we planning on visiting? "You're busy? The whole world is busy! It's not easy being old, Jennifer, and let me tell you something else, it ain't for sissies, and by the way, they've got a special on for pot roast at the Marriot." It was like having a nagging and very elderly uncle, only in this case, we weren't going to inherit anything when he died, as he did in the summer of 2001, leaving a hole in our lives. There were scores of fabulous, non-nutty, people, too, of course: the people who ran the religious school and organized luncheons, visited the sick and sat on the ritual committee. But it was only small-town Judaism of the type, no doubt, that many of my ancestors had experienced, particularly those on my mother's side who had settled in the mid-South. For the first time in my life, I felt that I was a part of a people, that I counted. *L'dor v'dor:* from generation to generation. Every Wednesday morning at ten, I sat with Rabbi Paul in the synagogue's library, slowly sounding out the Hebrew prayers while Paul, ever enthusiastic, told me that I was doing great, which actually wasn't even close to true, as I was a beginner, as unschooled as a chick. On Friday, in preparation for Shabbat, I made challah. I even started looking forward to services, if only so I could hang out afterward, schmoozing over the world's largest assortment of fattening foods. I was so at home in the synagogue that I found myself doing yoga in the synagogue library, and then helping myself to the contents of the synagogue's refrigerator. This was all new to me, and wonderful.

Then disaster struck. Rabbi Paul announced that he was leaving Baton Rouge, and Beth Shalom, for greener, and certainly more Jewish, pastures: Baltimore. Rabbi Paul was heading to a synagogue called Beth Am. But I knew better. Beth Am wasn't really Beth Am at all. It was merely a change in name: the congregation that Rabbi Paul was going to was the former Chizuk Amuno, where generations of my father's family had worshipped, and where I too had sat, year after year, dying of boredom and convinced that the rabbi, with his specially trained, X-ray vision, would see right through me, and discover that rather than read *Life at Camp Kee-Tov, The Story of Abraham,* and other classics of Sunday school literature, I spent my homework time busily rereading ancient Archie comic books and dreaming of the day that I'd have bosoms like Betty and Veronica. Chizuk Amuno—where I had spent one awful, interminable Rosh Hashanah crippled by a stomachache, where my father had become a bar mitzvah in 1942, my grandfather had become a bar mitzvah in 1889, and where my great-great grandfather, Michael Simon Levy, had served as a founding member and chairman of the committee that built the magnificent, austere structure that still stands on Eutaw Place. Chizuk

Amuno: the family shul, and site of some of my most painful childhood desolation.

Naturally, I took Paul's change of venue very personally. What right did he have to up and leave like that? Just up and leave, and just when I'd started—albeit in a kind of wishy-washy way—to study for my long-delayed bat mitzvah? It stunk. And it stunk even worse, because in his wake, Beth Shalom's search committee panicked and hired, as Paul's replacement, the first shnorrer to come round the bend, this little rabbit of a man, a nebbish who quickly alienated a good chunk of the congregation, which then set up a congregation-wide civil war.

I will not bore you with the details of the war that raged within the walls of Beth Shalom synagogue in Baton Rouge for more than two years before someone finally had the bright idea of hiring a new rabbi. But I will say this: as far as I was concerned, the soul had been sucked clear out of the joint. Right around the same time that the civil wars were raging, a new congregant, wearing a yarmulke and a long white beard, showed up. It didn't take long for people to notice that the new congregant, Charles, had an incredibly beautiful, powerful singing voice and that, as a bonus, he spoke fluent Hebrew (and a few additional languages besides, including Cajun French). Anyway, one day I decided that, in the absence of anything really going on in the synagogue, I may as well ask him if he could teach me to speak Hebrew. "Lama lo?" he said. (Why not?)

In fact "learn Hebrew" had been on my to-do list for years, but I never actually thought I'd take it up. After all, not only was I a Hebrew-school dropout, but also, my talent for languages is negligible at best. The language I should have learned—and which even now I kick myself for not having mastered—is Spanish, which I studied in high school, and then again for two years in college, in order to fulfill the college's language requirement. Unfortunately, because I had less motivation than an amoeba, I spent most of my class time writing very bad poetry. When I finally went to Spain after college, it was all I could do to ask for directions to the restroom.

But now, in Baton Rouge, I was having weekly Hebrew lessons.

"Hello. My name is Charles."

"Pleased to meet you. I am Jennifer."

"I like your house."

"I too like my house."

"Where are you from?"

"I'm from America."

"I too am from America. Where is your dog?"

"I don't have a dog."

"I have two dogs. Do you like dogs?"

"Yes."

"One of my dogs speaks Hebrew. The other speaks French."

"Hello."

"This is the truth."

It was the truth: Charles's two enormous black mastiffs spoke, respectively, Hebrew and French, with only a smattering of English between the two of them. In fact, the dog who spoke Hebrew spoke it considerably better than I did. After every lesson, I swore I'd quit. Half the time, I was so frustrated that I'd end up in tears and Stuart would have to calm me down, pointing out that no one would care whether or not I learned Hebrew and that even if I did, Hebrew wasn't a real useful language to have in South Louisiana.

But the truth was, I really did want to learn how to speak Hebrew, which really had been on my to-do list for a decade or so, and the reason I did was very simple: I wanted a language in which I could talk to my father, some secret code that he and I might share, a bridge of words and syntax and meaning that one day I might walk across, finding him waiting for me on the other side. After all, I thought, no one else was going to bother. My brother had married an Episcopalian and had, in short order, four distinctly half-and-half children, the eldest of whom was baptized. My younger sister, Amalie, who lived in Vermont, wasn't showing a whole lot of interest, either, and my older sister, Binky, when she wasn't working, was busy dating every last narcissistic asshole in the tri-state area, which sent our mother into fits of Jewish-mother angst the likes of which could have powered the combined forces of NATO and appeared to preclude any possibility that Binky might suddenly decide to change careers, abandoning the law for, say, a stint as a student at the Jewish Theological Seminary.

Along with chemotherapy, grades and types of tumors, my father's never-ending work habits, and Nana's descent into not-knowing, Binky's stubborn refusal to find some schmo or another and get married already became one of my mother's chief themes. In fact, during this time, Mom would call me, say, "What's new?" and before I'd had a chance to say, "Hi, Mom," launch into a diatribe of anxiety: Will Binky ever get married already my God she's almost forty and you know your sister's stubborn as a mule just like your father she works too hard too which is half of the problem right there how on earth is she going to meet someone nice if she's at the office all the time and even if she does meet someone, my God, you know Binky, she's so smart, she'll probably scare him off and by the way Jennifer, do you know anyone for her? You and Stuart have friends in New York, but, my God, Jennifer, and I don't want you ever to repeat this to your sister, do you understand, but after I die—and you have to make a promise—promise me that you won't ever let your sister be alone on the Jewish holidays, okay? No, I mean it, Jennifer, because in the end this cancer is going to win, and I'm all right with that, but I'm not all right with your sister being alone so promise me, I mean it.

"Good morning," Charles would say.

"Good morning."

"Would you like tea?"

"No. Please. The coffee is how I like."

"Black?"

"No, please, it is better with sugar and also with milk please thank you."

"Would you like to eat something?"

"I would like to eat eggs with juice that is very good."

"What do you want to do today here at the hotel?"

"I want to swim in the sea and sleep in my bed. I wear my bathing suit pretty and new from the market."

And so it went, week after week, month after month, reminding me, as much as anything, of the kind of conversations I'd been forced to endure during my dating years, before I'd met Stuart, and started talking with him so furiously it was as if we'd only just discovered the joys of spoken language. My mother once remarked that I married Stuart just so I'd have someone who had to listen to me. She also used to sit at the kitchen table late at night and tell me about her own father, her beloved father, Clarence, who had died in February of 1959, four months before I was born. "You would have loved him so much," she'd say. "He had such a twinkle in his eye." Then she would add, "When you grow up, I want you to marry a man like my father," and I would imagine this long-dead grandfather of mine, this kindly, sweet man whom I had never met and never would meet, as a kind of rumpled angel, in soft, worn khaki trousers, and a much-washed white button-down shirt. He'd be standing on the grass, his hands in his pockets, smiling. It wasn't until I was well into my forties that I realized how much my mother still missed him, how different all our lives would have been had my grandfather lived, how my mother's heart had never recovered, and would never recover, from his death, how bereft she felt, how unable to really love again, or at least not in the open-hearted, in-nocent, joyous way that she'd once loved her father.

My own father had continued to work as hard as ever, putting in hours that would break a man half his age, and then, on the weekends, doing battle with the great Virginia countryside, chopping wood, sawing off branches, mowing the enormous front lawn, raking, planting. Then he'd go inside, make sure that Mom was still breathing, and pick up where he'd left off with something entertaining, like David Hartman's *Love and Terror in the God Encounter: The Theological Legacy of Rabbi Joseph B. Soloveitchik*, or, if he were in the mood for something light, Kafka's later work or Amos Oz's contemporary fiction, in the original Hebrew.

Dad had started studying modern Hebrew at roughly the same age I started studying modern Hebrew: forty. Jerusalem had only just been re-unified, and for people like my father, who had grown up in an Orthodox household where both Judaism and the Jewish people were front and cen-ter, the sense of connection, optimism, and hope was intoxicating. That my father, in addition, had always been strong-willed is something of an understatement, and now he was determined to be able to kibbitz on the kibbutz. He'd sit for hours in the study of our house in McLean, studying his blue-and-white Hebrew textbook with a pencil in his hand.

My parents traveled to Israel for the first time in the summer of 1968, when I was nine. Along with Jews from all over the world, they longed to cast their gaze upon Jerusalem. Jerusalem—city of gold! They wandered through the ancient twisting streets of the Old City, with its heavy, heady smells of musk, citrus, tobacco smoke, oils and spices; they prayed at the Western Wall and visited the Dome of the Rock, the site of the *akedat* (the binding of Isaac), where Abraham's hand was stopped by the angel, and where the prophet Mohammed is said by the Koran to have taken his night journey: "From the sacred temple to the temple that is most remote" (Sura 17). And when they returned, a week or two later, they were filled with stories of this wondrous, magical land, this place of desert and mountain, of ancient olive groves and deeply shaded walled gardens, of kibbutzim filled with happy, healthy Jewish farmers and their extraordinarily beautiful children. They also brought us presents. Gold pendants for the girls; a prayer book for my brother. My own pendant was teardrop shaped and inscribed with flowers and Hebrew lettering spelling out the word *chai:* life. I still have it. Shortly afterward, my father started studying Hebrew.

What my father's impulses and motivations were, I can only guess— though at least a part of it had to do with his increasingly frequent trips to Jerusalem, where he had friends, and to Tel Aviv, where he had business. I suspect too that, like Jews all over the world, he was swept up with the romantic vision of the new Israeli Jew, the tanned pioneers who had turned the desert into a fruited garden, growing a Western-style democracy in the arid political soil of the tribal, bloody Middle East. In Israel, Jews wore sandals and open-necked shirts; they spoke a new, modern, incandescent Hebrew and built great universities; tilled the soil, ate hummus, and wrote literature in a language that was both as old as the Judean hills and as fresh as wind. A new people, born out of the ravages of the last war.

My own motivation was decidedly more mixed, particularly as I was coming at my studies with almost total Hebrew illiteracy, which my meetings with Rabbi Paul had done little to assuage.

Shalom. Shmi Yennifer. (Hello, my name is Jennifer.) *Ani mekavah ooga.* (I would like cake.)

Another reason I wanted to try Modern Hebrew was that I thought it would be a way into ancient, biblical, and prayer-book Hebrew, the love poetry that my ancestors had written to God. And perhaps, I thought, in this way, I too might walk the Jewish path, the halacha to God. I knew I'd never have the patience to sit in a classroom (or elsewhere) and decipher biblical grammar and syntax. But a spoken, vibrant language—one in which you can say *ani ohevet min* (I love sex) or *ha nasi hoo kol kach tipish she ani rotza l'hakey* (the president is so stupid that I'm going to throw up)—seemed doable. But the most compelling reason for me to tackle Hebrew in my middle years was the image of my father sitting in his study, his Hebrew textbook open on his lap, a pencil in his hand as he conjugated reflexive verbs.

One day, I worked up all my nerve, called my father, and said: *Abba, ata yodeah sh ani lomedet Evrit mipneshe rotzati sfa m'yuhad v parati ledeber itcha?* (You do know, Daddy, that I am studying Hebrew because I wanted to have a special private language to talk to you in?)

My father said: *Bividai, biti, ani yodae.* (Of course I know, my daughter.)

By the time our synagogue finally hired a new rabbi, I was a year or so into my Hebrew studies, and though I could hardly chatter away like a *sabre* (a native-born Israeli), or even like a newly minted Russian immigrant in Tel Aviv, I was beginning to get into it.

In any event, our new rabbi, Stan Zamek, was married to Martha Bergadine, also a rabbi, giving Beth Shalom two rabbis with one change of personnel. Rabbis Stan and Martha moved to Baton Rouge in July. I fell so in love with both of them that I felt like a groupie. (This was around the time that Stuart started telling people, "Jennifer has a thing for rabbis.") It was at this time, too, that I had my crisis in faith, and, returning home from Maine, I practically threw myself at Rabbi Stan's feet. "The notion of God is just a big game we play on ourselves!" I wailed one early evening in the Beth Shalom parking lot, as my kids, sitting in the back seat of my minivan, gestured impatiently for me to finish up already and take them home for dinner. "A mere byproduct of evolution!" And on and on I went, until at last Stan put a hand on my shoulder, saying: "It's okay. Faith is hard." He then suggested that I join the class he planned to teach on Abraham Joshua Heschel's seminal *God in Search of Man,* a book that, in a nutshell, posits that God is lonely, yearning for connection with His human children, that He'd spoken and continues to speak through the biblical prophets, and that the very question concerning the existence or nonexistence of God points to relationship. Later, in class, Rabbi Stan would read a particularly hard snippet, we'd all take a stab at what it meant, and then Stan would explain it to us. One day, I confessed how, as a child, I'd gone to God on a regular basis, as a kind of insurance policy, laying out all my boo-boos, and begging Him to protect me and my family from an infinite number of potential calamities. People were looking at me like I was a total weirdo, but after I was done, everyone else chimed in, describing his or her personal theology. It was sort of like ontological group therapy. Rabbi Stan said that I'd gotten it right the first time, and I felt so good that it was as if I had just ingested some wonderful new illegal drug.

Meanwhile, Charles and I met every Wednesday night:

"Perhaps, my teacher, I am so stupid that my head, she is full of stupidness."

"You lack self-confidence."

"I lack ability for being the smart, this is problem of me. The words, they are falling out of my ears. They are falling onto the table made of wood."

"Do you want to hear a joke?"

"I am wanting."

"Why are Jews so smart?"

"Why?"

"Because they go to concentration camps."

"Yes to please say again please excuse me?"

Later, when my frustration with Hebrew was at an all-time peak, I approached Rabbi Stan outside his office and said, "Would you please explain to me why on earth I am spending all this time learning a language that I probably will never use and moreover is written in an alphabet that goes the wrong way?" He gazed at me for a second, put his hand on my shoulder, and said, "Because it's the language of your people."

5|

Holy Ghost

Valerie had been lying up in her bed at St. Anthony's for a year or two before I finally took notice of her and started visiting. Not that I'd been unaware of her presence before, it was just that I usually spent the morning that I had allotted as my volunteer time either with Philomena or driving people around, and Valerie—who had been dumped at St. Anthony's two or three years after my "first generation" had died—wasn't expected to last much longer. So why bother? She was totally out-of-it, anyway, barely able to frame a single thought into words, and so fat she could barely move. But Val was as beautiful as she was big. She had a regal face, with high cheekbones, lovely, almond-shaped eyes, and a full mouth. Every day, the caregivers would give her a sponge bath and then fix her hair, pulling it into a tight little ponytail at the top of her head, while she rolled her eyes and babbled. She babbled on about this and that—how the man at the school had hurt her and her father who was coming tomorrow for her birthday and the fireman who kept trying to climb into her window and her newborn daughter—and not only did none of it make any kind of linear, logical, narrative sense, but also, I could barely understand a word she said. She talked without punctuation, without intonation, and without pause, her words all running together. And it wasn't as if I could really *do* anything for her, anyway. I couldn't even read to her, as her mind no longer tracked. Philomena was one thing, but I just wasn't sure that I could take Valerie. In any event, I way preferred the guys—especially Victor, who had moved in around the same time that Val had and had quickly become the senior resident, the head man. How can I describe Victor without sounding like a Hallmark card? It was hard for me to imagine him in his former incarnation as a hardened junkie, because by the time he started to feel well enough to peel himself up off his bed and hang around with the other residents at St. Anthony's, he was wide-open all over. His face was wide-open, his eyes were wide-open, and his heart was, too. You could feel it coming off of him, this wide-open quality he had, this happy curiosity, as if he couldn't get over his amazement that he was still alive. When his face broke out into a grin, you could feel happiness radiating from him in the same kind of pure white smile that very young children have before school and other kids and TV and disappointed unhappy parents and all the rest of it rob them of their inborn sense of all-rightness. Except, of course, that Victor was no child but a man in his late thirties, with a personal history that sounded like the lyrics of an over-the-top rap song. He'd go on and on about how he'd been scraped up out of the gutter by a kind and merciful Jesus, his ass hauled over to Earl K. Long while he was still half out of his mind and emaciated and just about dead, didn't deserve no nothing after the life he'd lived, the life on the street, had himself a job and a wife and a nice place to live, but no, he just has to go chasing that one pure high, that one last high that was going to be his last, only with him the last never did come, because the high came before everything else, before his wife (who left him) and his kids (who left with their mother), before his job (he'd once been a long-distance truck driver), even before his own mamma and daddy, the parents who had raised him up right, raised him up to know right from wrong—and it was his own damn fault what had happened to him, hell he was lucky he *only* had AIDS, what with the shit he'd done. And he'd talk on and on like that, telling me about his life on the street, his life from Before—Before he'd found Jesus, Before God had given him a chance to straighten himself out, saving his skin so that he could get his strength back at St. Anthony's and no ma'am, he was done with that shit, that shit can kill you, that shit *will* kill you. He'd tell me about his friends in Scotlandville, where he'd grown up, only they weren't really his friends, they were his drug-friends, the people he got high with, only, shit, they'd just as soon have killed him for a ten-dollar bill as left him alone, it's a miracle he never *was* killed, he had to sleep with his eyes open in those days, because if he shut them, well then, he might just wake up dead. All over a ten-dollar bill. I would drive him to one or the other of his sisters' houses, both in spanking-new subdivisions of modest, neat brick houses in the middle of a field in the middle of nowhere on the far eastern edge of the parish, and he'd tell me about them, how both of them had grown up to be schoolteachers. "Smart," he'd say. "Never did give up on me don't know why." He told me about a friend who he'd come up with, known him since they were little, getting in trouble together, only his friend, one day, he was found dead with a needle in his arm, dead on the kitchen floor and the whole house stinking like garbage, like infestation, like rot, and no, sir, that is not how he, Victor, wanted to end up.

Before he up and spiked a fever and took sick and died in the intensive care ward at Earl K. Long with tubes sticking in him and machines beeping and buzzing near his head, Victor's friend Earl told stories too. Earl was a big guy—six foot one or two—and built solid. He wore the same kind of loose-weave, short-sleeved cotton shirts that Stuart buys every year from the Eddie Bauer catalog, and brown leather sandals, and though his eyesight was bad—he wore thick glasses—he could sit for hours on the sofa in the front room, watching horror movies, which he rented by the cartload at Blockbuster's. Movies with titles like *Death Freak II, Saturday Night Blood,* or *Ripper.* He was insatiable. He walked slowly, with deliberation, and had a certain grace about him too, as if maybe in a former life he'd been a monk or the head of an elite boys' boarding school. So there was Earl, who liked to go to the Blockbuster to get movies, and Victor, who liked to go just about anywhere, and between the two of them they kept me pretty busy, which was just fine, because even though I hated schlepping around Baton Rouge, I liked being with Victor and Earl. Driving past the Carpet King, past Donut Heaven, past the Home Depot and Don's Seafood and the hardware store and the McDonald's and the industrial canal they cut down there to divert water from the river if it ever rains again, which these days seems unlikely—we're in a drought and the whole damn state seems to be drying up, the lakes shrinking and getting covered over with rancid brown algae—we talk and laugh. Being with them was sort of like being with the two older brothers I never had, the brothers who are always on your side even while they tease you about everything from the way you wear your hair to the boy you have a crush on.

But Valerie was always there, lying in bed, around the corner from Philomena's room. As I walked by, I could see her, her eyes half-rolled back in her head, talking to herself. Sometimes I'd stop and sit with her for a minute or two, but frankly, I didn't have the patience. *Hi, Valerie, it's me, Jennifer, I've come for a visit. Who you say you are? I'm Jennifer. I volunteer here. I've come for a visit. You Jennifer? You sure you not Joanna? I'm Jennifer. I volunteer here. You the white girl? That's right. Well Jennifer how come I don't see you before?* And then she'd be off and running, talking about her age—which sometimes was twenty-one and other times was sixteen and still other times was closer to her real age, thirty-seven—and her ex-husband who was a no-good man, and all kinds of other stuff, but I only caught every third or fourth word, and that was on a good day. I'd sit there for five or ten minutes waiting for a break in her monologue so I could say goodbye and slip out.

Out with the guys, who were fun to be with, and who told stories. Earl's story about how one time he'd gone over to his girlfriend's house only she'd put all his things out in the yard, all his shirts and shoes, his neckties, his socks, even his toothbrush, and why? Because he had him another woman, that's why, it wasn't no sin, it was the way of men, and if she didn't like it . . . oooo she was mad! And Earl's going on like this, about how mad and bad and evil women could be, and then I join in the fray too, calling him a low-down, scumbag, cheating two-timer, no wonder his girlfriend threw him out, what did he expect, he was lucky none of his women friends hadn't taken a shot at him. Which made Victor and Earl laugh so hard the car shook. Victor's story about the first time he'd seen snow, it was when he was still driving long distances, went all the way out to the state of Washington, and it was summer, but there was snow in the mountains; he never had seen anything like it before, those beautiful mountains glowing in the sun.

One day I was about to head out the door with Earl and Victor. Victor wanted to go get new socks and a pair of jeans. Earl wanted to go to some mom-and-pop sandwich shop that he knew about on Gus Young Avenue, near the railroad tracks, you know, Jennifer, you never been to Frank's? (Katz's delicatessen, yes; Frank's, no.) Victor wanted to go to his sister's house, too. And that's when Philomena came padding out of her room on her two swollen, bad legs, wearing an LSU purple-and-gold T-shirt and shorts, and saying that she wanted to join us.

Caroline was the caregiver on duty that day. She took Philomena aside and said: "Philomena, honey, you wearing your diaper? Because you knows you just took your fluid pill and if you wants to go out with Jennifer then you can't be having no accidents."

Philomena said, "I am fine. I have taken care of myself."

"You sure?"

"I am not a child."

Caroline went back into the caregiver's station—a little room off the lounge where the staff keeps the meds under lock and key, keeps track of medication schedules, and stashes Band-Aids and Neosporin and cough medicine and Tylenol—shaking her head and saying, "All right then, just so long as you sure."

Off we went, up and over the railroad tracks, past the new Winn Dixie and the railroad yards, past the community center, past the Glen Oaks apartments where they'd had all those murders recently, past the new Pine Glory housing complex, past some boarded-up storefronts and shotguns and a bunch of empty parking lots fanning out in front of empty big-box stores, former Wal-Marts and former Albertsons grocery stores and former Mattress Wholesalers and a former Discount City, block after block of abandoned warehouses, block after block of asphalt football fields stretching along the side of the road—America after a nuclear holocaust. We rounded a corner: Shotgun shacks, broken sidewalks, modest wooden houses with the paint peeling off, chain-link fences, scraggly trees, kids. Where Earl knew some folks. Where he had to go see this fellow. "Fellow who work at the liquor store. No, Jennifer, I ain't doing no drug deal or nothing else like that. Just got to talk to the fellow, that's all. He know me. Been knowing me too, for a long time. Just got to talk to him and I know that's where he works and I can't call him because I don't know where he's been staying." So I pulled up to the liquor store and Earl got out and we sat there in the car for a while and then he came back, which was when it was time to take Victor to the Dollar Store: "Won't take but a little while if you don't mind, Jennifer, I sure would like to get me some new jeans."

Some time in between stopping for Earl's friend at the liquor store and shopping for blue jeans at the Dollar Store, Philomena started complaining that she had to go to the bathroom. The problem was, there was no bathroom. No bathroom at the liquor store; no bathroom at the Dollar Store. In fact, outside restaurants, gas stations, and shopping malls, a public bathroom in Baton Rouge is hard to come by. By now we were in a particularly bleak area, stretching between two truck routes and plagued by abandoned houses and long-empty storefronts, a place with virtually no services. "Take me to a gas station," Philomena said, but there were no gas stations. "Take me to a McDonald's," she said, but there were no McDonald's. Earl said he knew of a place just up ahead, a neighborhood grocery store, and she could probably go there. By the time I pulled up to park, Philomena was holding her crotch and rocking back and forth, tears and sweat running down her face. I opened Philomena's door, slung one of her arms over my shoulders, and started half-dragging her, half-coaxing her into the grocery store, and then we were in the grocery store and I asked a clerk where the bathroom was please my friend isn't feeling well—and he pointed us toward the back, but I was too late. I heard Philomena's pee hitting the floor, and looked down to see a dark puddle spreading on the old, oily, wide wooden planks. "I'm so sorry," she whispered. I don't remember what I said in return, but at last we managed to get to the small, windowless bathroom in the back of the store, behind the boxes in a storage hall. I left her there to go and grab a towel that I happened to have in the back of my car. When she came out of the bathroom, Philomena was wrapped in the towel, wearing it like a tribal skirt.

When we returned to St. Anthony's, Caroline scolded Philomena for having been so pigheaded, going out without a diaper like she had. But it was my fault. I'm not saying that to be noble, it's simply a fact. I was so caught up with the guys—with the idea of myself hanging out with the brothers—that I ignored Philomena until it was too late.

Philomena died a couple of months later, while I was at my parents' summer house in Maine. I'd sent her a postcard with a picture of a moose on it, but she died before it arrived. When I returned to St. Anthony's in late August, Miss Dolly told me that Philomena's funeral had been beautiful. It had been at the Nigerian church, she said, and hundreds of people had turned out to say goodbye. (I had been unaware, until then, that there was any such entity as the Nigerian church in Baton Rouge.) Then she looked up at me and said: "Who knew?"

In Philomena's darkened, empty room was a single memorial candle. I sat there for a little while, looking at the window, and trying to feel some whiff of Philomena, some sense of her being hovering in the corners or tickling my skin. But there was nothing. When I emerged from the room a minute later, Valerie heard my footsteps and called out to me, calling for me to come and visit.

Maybe next week, I said, hurrying along, hurrying and scurrying, because I had to get back home, to my real life, to my computer, and my work, and all the thousand-and-one things I have to do in order for the world to keep functioning, there's my endless to-do list and my three kids' piano lessons and soccer games and homework and speech therapy appointments, my garden that needs weeding. And I have my Hebrew studies as well, including my bat mitzvah, which I'm going forward with again, this time with Rabbi Stan, for reasons that even I don't fully understand, and let's face it, I'm in a complete, heart-racing panic over my entire life, because even though I come here every Tuesday morning like clockwork, even though I'm as reliable as the sun, I always feel like I'm racing the clock and that if I don't prevail, I will be sucked under: me, my hopes, my ambitions, my dreams, all of it just drowning in a sea of mediocrity and failure, of never-good-enoughness, and frankly, there's just something about Valerie, something about her near-blindness, and her size, and her need—her complete dependence on others—that makes me uncomfortable. Or maybe it's just that it's so boring to be with her. It's like being with a baby, but worse, because you can rock a baby in your arms, sing to it, inhale its shining new innocence into your nostrils. What was I supposed to do with a 280-pound dying woman who couldn't keep the basic facts of her own life straight? Since when had I been elected to save the world?

Joanna—the same caregiver who taught me to ask for God's help not only in times of need, but always, and especially whenever I sit down at the computer—liked to sing. Every now and then, she'd bring her electric keyboard to work, set it up in the front room, and really let loose. She did all the classics: "I Will Be Joyful," "I Know the Lord Will Make a Way," "Still I Rise," "You Brought Me," and anything else that anyone asked for. She'd sit there in the living room, just letting it rip, her full voice rich and expressive, her face shining, and you'd have to be an idiot not to see that every cell of her body was filled with music. Typically, when Joanna began to sing, all the other women would join in too, but for some reason, the men tended to stay away, and when one or two of them did appear, they'd hover at the edges of the room, like teenage boys at their first dance. I think there was something about the emotionality of Joanna's singing that made them slightly uncomfortable. It was either that or the sight of the skinny white volunteer sitting on the sofa bawling.

I can't help it. Just about any time I hear gospel music, I tear up, and when I hear the real thing, live and in person, I'm a goner. But it pisses me off, too, because here I am, one of the gang, I've paid my dues, crossed over, left my résumé behind, but I can't join in. And I can't join in for one very simple reason: I can't sing. My voice is utterly useless.

I can't sing because neither of my parents can sing, and my father's voice is so bad that it's painful. My voice isn't quite as bad as my father's, but unlike Dad, who, in addition to his thin, reedy, off-key voice, also has a tin ear, I can *hear.* Thus when I sing, and my voice veers off-key (as it inevitably does by the third or fourth beat) I can hear how awful I sound. Very early in life, I learned to fake it, mouth the words, let my own voice be drowned out in the surrounding swell of other children's harmonics.

One day, I walk into St. Anthony's to find Valerie propped up in a recliner in the front room, her hair pulled up in a little topknot like a Chinese emperor, her enormous arms resting on pillows. Joanna has brought her keyboard, and all the other women have gathered around. I can hear each woman's voice distinctly, and as usual, I'm filled with this gooey combination of yearning and envy. How I wish I could sing like that! How I wish I could open my lips and—in the words of the prayer the precedes the *Amida* (one of Judaism's most central prayers)—*Open my mouth and my lips shall declare God's glory!* But it's not to be. My lips might open, but what comes out is frog croaks.

What comes out of Valerie's mouth, on the other hand, *is* glory: her voice is thin but strong. It flits in and out, warbling, caressing each word. She sings from her chair with her head thrown back and her eyes closed, and if you didn't know any better, you'd swear you were hearing the voice of an angel.

"You got the Holy Ghost, Val," Joanna tells her afterward, and I wonder: if I pray hard enough, or with the right concentration—the *kavanah* of intentionality that the rabbis speak of—will God let me sing too? After all, if He's omniscient, omnipotent, and omnipresent, like He's cracked up to be, then sending me a melodious voice shouldn't be any big deal. He divided the Red Sea, went before Israel in a cloud, and helped Daniel find his way out of the lion's den. Surely He can replace my deficient pipes with shiny new copper ones.

My father raised us on stories of the great cantor Josef Abba Weisgal, who presided over services in Baltimore at Chizuk Amuno in the good old days, when Dad was a boy and the shul was packed, not like it is today, kids, but I mean packed: the balconies were full, and downstairs, especially on the holidays, it would be standing-room only!

Abba had been trained in Poland, Germany, and eventually Vienna before coming to America shortly after the First World War. The story I was told was that when my grandfather, Leslie, "auditioned" him for the *chazzan's* job at Chizuk Amuno, Abba sang opera selections in German for over an hour. He got the job. Moreover, he was still at it when I was a child. Whenever we went to Baltimore, for Rosh Hashanah or Passover, or just because Dad felt like it, Abba's emotionally rich voice continued to fill the lovely old synagogue, floating up over the heads of the aging, frail congregants and pushing against the ceiling. By then, of course, Abba was an old man, and his voice had lost much of its strength. Even so, my father got all teary-eyed every time he heard him, and though he may well be the most tone-deaf person ever born, he'd go into ecstasies of appreciation over the beauty of the service and the power of the music. Years later, he wrote that "when Abba chanted the prayers it was as though the history of the Jewish people was being recreated in your presence with all its beauty and sadness, hopes and disappointments." But as a kid, I didn't get it. To me, the tunes seemed weird, all in these keening minor tones, like something from beyond the grave or someplace else that you really didn't want to think about too much. As far as I could tell, there wasn't much in the way of melody at all, and what melody you could latch onto was hardly of the hand-clapping, finger-snapping variety. All in all, I preferred the Monkees. Plus—what was *with* my father, anyway? Most of the time, I believed myself to be invisible before him, and on those rare occasions that he managed to register my existence, I was fairly sure that he wasn't all that crazy about what he saw. Versus what happened at that dreary old synagogue of his, where his heart melted and he turned to mush. Before my eyes, he went from being Mr. Tough Guy to Captain Sentimental.

In any event, I always associated Jewish music with what I heard in Baltimore, and I never understood why we, the people who had given the world Leonard Bernstein, André Previn, and James Levine, not to mention Isaac Stern and Itzhak Perlman, hadn't come up with our own version of gospel music. Then my father invited me to join him in Romania, where he had been invited to join the Romanian Yiddish Youth Choir on its annual Hanukkah tour. It was the winter of 1984. I was twenty-five.

How I ended up tagging along with my father—who himself was tagging along—on a Romanian Yiddish Youth Choir Hanukkah tour is a bit of a long story involving, among other things, international relations, the U.S. Senate, the history of Eastern European anti-Semitism, and my psychoanalyst, Dr. Abrams. The short version, however, is that Romania's long-time and deeply anti-Semitic dictator, Nicolae Ceaușescu, had granted the country's dwindling Jewish community a fair amount of autonomy (including the right to emigrate to Israel) and the Romanian Jewish community, under the direction of its brilliant chief rabbi, David Rosen, responded by organizing kosher kitchens, old-age homes, and a Yiddish youth choir. Every year, the choir traveled from town to town, singing in ancient, unheated, wooden synagogues to the mainly impoverished, mainly elderly Jews who'd remained in the shtetl after the war. It was a big media event, the idea being that if Ceaușescu could show off his liberal policies toward his Jewish subjects, he'd demonstrate to the powerful Jews who control America that his government was worthy of receiving certain beneficial trade breaks from the United States. My father, who had long been a *macher* (mover and shaker) in various American Jewish organizations, was invited to attend, and asked me and my sister Amalie, who was then just out of college, if we'd like to go too.

The chance to go to Romania in the dead of winter with my father, who still terrified me, and a bunch of Communist Iron Guardsmen armed with Soviet machine guns didn't at first appeal to me. Then I spent a week or two obsessing about whether or not I should go, telling Dr. Abrams about all the mean things that people had done to me when I was little, and freaking out over a dream I'd had about snakes, until finally, one night, Dad called and said, "Why *wouldn't* you come, Jen? When are you ever going to have another chance like this?" Dr. Abrams agreed, so I got my passport renewed, packed Grandma Etta's ancient, ratty sealskin coat, and flew, with my father, from JFK to Vienna, where we boarded another plane, this one held together with Band-Aids, and flew into Bucharest. The streets were filthy; the people were pale and pasty and thin; even well-fed people somehow looked rabbity, as if they'd never met a vegetable or seen the sun. The entire country appeared to have recently been bull-dozed to make room for Stalinist monstrosities—giant, gray boxes made of cinderblock—and empty, garbage-strewn lots.

The next day, we met up with Rabbi Rosen, who was then well into his eighties, but vigorous and formidable, with the large, suffering, soulful eyes of a tsaddik and the long white beard of a prophet. Dressed in a som-ber, dark suit, a yarmulke on his head, Rabbi Rosen was a figure straight out of a lost world, that vast Ashkenazi civilization that had disappeared in Hitler's ovens. During the war, he'd been among the tens of thousands of Romanian Jews forced on a barefoot death march across the countryside in the dead of winter. He'd been repeatedly beaten up by successive fascist paramilitary groups, starved, imprisoned, and left for dead. But he stal-wartly refused to die. He was a brilliant and wily old man who spoke He-brew, Yiddish, Romanian, Russian, Italian, French, Polish, and English, whose mission had become to get every last member of Romania's dwin-dling and dying Jewish community to Israel.

"Hello," he said to me, taking me in with one glance and dismissing me with what looked to me like a little internal shrug, as if he could tell that I spent the better part of my days either obsessing about my love life or weeping on an analytical couch on the Upper East Side.

The next day the entire entourage, including our Communist keepers, our CIA watchdogs, a goodly chunk of the Israeli Knesset, and Rabbi Rosen himself boarded a bus, which took us north into the bleak brown December landscape, toward towns that were no longer on any map, with names that the Communist regime had long since blotted out, and were now remembered only by a few elderly Jews: Falticeni, Todorccha, Sole-shiu, Piatre, Tirgu-Mures, Baccau, Timisora, and Pietra Neamt, where it is said that the Ba'al Shem Tov—the "Master of the Good Name" who founded the Hasidic movement—prayed. I sat next to the window, looking out at a brown, wet, frozen landscape, at the face of misery: huts made out of corrugated tin and rotten wood, kids dressed in rags, Communist-style apartment buildings with sagging foundations and nonworking plumbing, women walking through the mud with buckets in their hands to get water from a pump. Everywhere we went, people stared, as if they'd never seen such wonders.

"Just wait until you hear these kids sing," Dad said. "You're not going to believe your ears."

Now the thing is, there was not one shred of Yiddishkeit culture in the house I grew up in. And that's because my ancestors were German Jews, products of the Haskala (or Enlightenment) that in the late eighteenth and early nineteenth centuries drew a fault line between the increasingly fervent Orthodox and Hasidim of Poland and Lithuania and the self-styled European Jews—enlightened citizens of an enlightened world—in Germany and Western Europe. On my mother's side, Haskala attitudes had permitted first the embrace of the new, streamlined Reform movement and then the pinnacle of pure American style that my mother's mother embodied—Judaism, and Jewishness, by default only. But even on my father's side of the family, where the traditional, Orthodox form of religion still held sway, Yiddish culture, and the vibrant, expressive Yiddish language that was the *carrier* of that culture, was not only not a part of the lexicon but also not part of the collective memory. My grandparents on both sides wouldn't have used a Yiddish expression if their lives had depended on it. Yiddish was vulgar—the language of rubes and rustics, of ignoramuses and nincompoops. It was an embarrassing reminder of who our people had once been, back in the European Diaspora: a whole race of weak, stateless, despised people, figures of fun, ignorant itinerant peasants and hapless farmers who froze to death in winter and were lucky to live into middle age. In our house, therefore, there were no *oy veys,* no *schlemiels,* no *putzes.* (It would take Leo Rosten, and the publication of his wildly popular *The Joys of Yiddish* in 1968, to begin to change American Jewish attitudes about Yiddish from shame to pride.) It wasn't until she was well into her sixties, and fighting cancer, that my mother started saying things like, "What a schnook," or "Your father, he's really messhuggeneh."

Yet here I was, sitting next to my meshuggeneh father on a Romanian bus heading north to the Moldovian border to hear a Romanian youth choir sing old Yiddish songs to a handful of elderly Jews in towns so small that they were no longer on the map. And there, in freezing-cold wooden synagogues with fancifully restored, brightly painted interiors, the elderly survivors of wars, forced marches, death camps, famines, and Communism came in their ratty winter coats, wearing old woolen caps, to sit on hard wooden benches and listen. The choir stood before the haphazard congregations and belted out all the biggies from a time long gone, that time before World War Two, when the thousand-year-old European Jewish community still thought that in the end, love and reason would prevail over blood-lust and race hatred. "Ovnt Lid," "Zayt Gezunt," "Ver Es Hot," "Ikh Shtey Unter a Bokserboym," "Roumania," "My Yiddishke Mama." The music was solemn, sweet, joyous, and playful by turns, and though I couldn't understand the lyrics, I could feel their meaning in my bones. Huddling together for warmth, visibly decrepit and seemingly ancient men and women wept openly, and next to me, on our wooden bench, the tears cascaded down my father's face. Again with the tears! Only this time, I was crying too. I just didn't want Dad to see me.

The Ba'al Shem Tov didn't write down his teachings; rather, he uttered them to disciples who in turn wrote them down. One of his disciples, Tanya, Shneur Zalman, wrote: "He alone is in the upper and lower worlds just as He was before the six days of Creation . . . when one reflects deeply on this, his heart will rejoice and his soul will be glad with joy and singing, with all his hearing and soul and might, in this superb faith, for this is the very experience and nearness of God." Nachman of Bratslav said: "Through song and joy, one can 'pour out his words like water in the presence of the Lord.'" And then there's the *Amida* with its plea that God allow the worshipper to declare His glories. But I never could quite declare, let alone sing, His glory without feeling dumb.

Please dear God let me sing.

Please dear God let me sing.

Please dear God I know it's kind of stupid, I know that my genes are my genes, but since You're God, and can do what You want to do, would You please help me out here, and put music in my mouth?

Dear God, get real—my voice sucks. Please give me a new one.

Please, God, I know that You have bigger things on Your mind, but if I could, at the very least, carry a tune, I sure would appreciate it.

Dear God, I am grateful to You for my manifold blessings, but if You could just add one more to the pile, and give me a singing voice, I will sing Your praises day and night, or at least when I remember to.

And while You're at it, Lord of All, would You please take the lump out of my chest, the one that holds all my envy and jealousy and sense that other people have it better? Because for God's sake, God, even after years of therapy, I'm really not that different from my best friend in high school, who was beautiful and radiant and sunny and gifted, who looked like a cross between a gazelle and a supermodel, but who loved drugs so much that eventually she gave her whole life to them, extinguishing her inner flame, sacrificing everything for chemical ecstasy. Let's face it, God and God of my Fathers, I'm a bit like that, only it's not drugs I'm addicted to. No, I've got the Jewish disease—or maybe just my family's version of it, or maybe just my own. Success—the golden fleece—and not just any old success, but a certain kind of flaming, extraordinary, and very public success, or you don't exist at all. Let me give it up! Because I know that nothing I accomplish in this world can possibly be more important than simply learning how to love. I even admit that I've done okay in life, that I have work that gives me satisfaction, that I married a good, kind man, and together we are teaching our children to be the people they are meant to be. The cup isn't half full. It's *more* than half full. Even so, sometimes I get so depressed, so weary, so convinced of my own total mediocrity—the girl who was buried on the bayou, sucked under by the swamps—that I have to Google myself to make sure I'm still alive.

I never did learn to sing. But nearly twenty years after I went with my father to Romania, and two years after Joanna at St. Anthony's told me that I needed to ask God to be with me in my work, I picked up a paintbrush and began to paint again for the first time since high school. What happened was that one day, when she was about eight, my daughter, Rose, asked me to get her some art stuff. I did so, and the next day, a Saturday, Rose decided to get her new art supplies out and began to paint a garden. After about ten minutes, she got bored, but by then I was in a fever.

While she'd been putting the finishing touches on her daisy, I'd been seized with a desire to make a picture of life at St. Anthony's. It took me two days. I cut out photographs of some of the residents and glued them on, affixing wings and halos to them. Earl was in the sky, with a halo, as was Philomena, and Gerald, and Little Chuck. I cut tinfoil into the shape of a cross and glued that on too. Then I wrote: "Joanna has met God face to face, but I just try to listen." As great art goes, it didn't exactly rate, but I was pleased with it, and the next time I went to St. Anthony's, I presented it to the residents, and Victor took it and hung it in the hall. After that, the images just started coming to me, as if from the sky.

"You've got the Holy Ghost, girl," Joanna said when she saw what I'd done.

I loved the idea of the Holy Ghost so much that I felt kind of guilty, having it, if indeed that's what comes over me when I'm face-to-face with a box of paints. I mean, *inspiration* is one thing, but the Holy Ghost, let's face it, just isn't kosher. But perhaps, I thought, my mother had had the Holy Ghost too—or at least she had before she got sick and started spending the better part of her days lying on the sofa and, when she was feeling up to it, planning her funeral down to the last detail, worrying about Binky, and generally concocting ways to drive me absolutely batshit. After all, what else could account for her wildly high spirits, the way she'd danced us around the house to the soundtrack of Zero Mostel's *Fiddler on the Roof* or, for that matter, just about any music that predated 1968? Perhaps *all* the Whitehills, wishy-washy Judaism or no, were infected.

Finally, I bit the bullet and asked Rabbi Stan, choosing my words carefully so he wouldn't think I'd gone over to the other side.

"The Holy Ghost?" he said.

I nodded.

"We don't actually call it that," he continued, "but we do believe in the joyousness of serving God. We call it the *Shechinah,* the Joy of Israel."

I thanked him and left.

6 |

The Memory Books

My mother continued to plan her death. She was writing letters to each of the grandchildren, so they'd have something to remember her by. She was compiling the family recipes, so that each of us would know how to make Grandma's pot roast and Nana's fruit-filled meringue. She was dividing up her jewelry—did I want her diamond and ruby necklace? What about her sapphire ring? And by the way, isn't there someone you can think of for your sister? I'm not going to last much longer, you know.

But it was bullshit, and I can say that with authority, because God just wasn't ready for Mom—not yet, at least. Even I, with all my doubts and dark corners about the very existence of the Almighty, knew that if He had any sense at all, He wouldn't be in any hurry to meet her up close and personal. Who could blame Him? She was so bossy she would have gotten to heaven and started rearranging the furniture. Unlike in the beautiful, stirring gospel number "I'm Too Close," which expresses the yearning to give up the struggle and surrender to death, my mother didn't have the slightest longing to see her God's face. The top of the hill? Forget it. She liked living in the broad green valleys. The next world? She liked the one she knew, the one where you could get a big, juicy hamburger and slather it with ketchup and relish, or sneak out of the house for lobster, which is strictly forbidden under the laws of kashrut—laws my mother had taken up when she married my father and ignored as much as possible thereafter. And though she probably didn't think of it that way, my mother's orientation toward both her life and her death was very Jewish, for in Judaism the material world with all its sensual splendors is as much a part of God's glory as the most distant stars, and, what's more, it's only through the material world, the everyday world of talking on the phone and going to the grocery store, enjoying a good cup of coffee or rocking out to the Rolling Stones, or perhaps Bruce Springsteen, that divinity can be glimpsed. She kept talking about dying, but instead of dying, she got fat.

A few months before my bat mitzvah, Mom called me, again, to talk about her impending death and the kind of flowers she wanted on her casket, but then she switched subjects, telling me that she was sending me a just-because present, one of the zillions of presents that my mother has given me over the years for no reason whatsoever other than because she felt like it: because she happened to be in Bloomingdale's or because she knew I could use a new coat, or a quilt covered with pastel-colored hearts, or an antique dining-room table with eight early-American ladder-back chairs. Sometimes (as in the case of the dining-room table and chairs) I liked the stuff she gave me; sometimes I didn't; but always, and no matter what, her extravagant gift-giving filled me with a sense of queasy guilt, which would then lead to a bout of hypochondria, wherein, usually in the space of two or three days, I'd develop the warning signs of AIDS, as well as numerous cancers.

"You'll like it."

"Thank you," I said, already feeling burdened by it—whatever it was.

But when the just-because present arrived a few days later, it turned out to be Nana's "Memory Books"—scrapbooks I'd pored over when I was a girl and which for years had been stored in the corner cabinet in my mother's sitting room. My mother had also sent me a note. It read: "Because I know that you will keep Mother's memories for her." I unwrapped the packages slowly, so as not to cause further damage to the brittle, yellowed pages.

In Judaism, there are prayers for everything: There is the blessing over fragrances, *Blessed art Thou, Our Lord and God, King of the universe, Who creates species of fragrance;* the blessing to be recited upon smelling herbs and spices, *Blessed art Thou, Our Lord, our God, King of the universe, Who creates herbage;* the blessing recited upon hearing thunder, *Blessed art Thou, Our Lord, our God, King of the universe, for his strength and his power fill the universe;* and my favorite, the blessing that is recited upon seeing unusually odd-looking people, *Blessed are Thou, Our Lord, our God, King of the universe, Who has made the creatures different.* There's a beautiful prayer for those who are setting out beyond the city limits, and because I am terrified of flying, convinced, as I always am, that the flight I'm on will be my last, I usually ask Rabbi Stan to bless me in the words of the Wayfarer's Prayer before I go anywhere. There are others, too: the one for the deliverance of a loved one from a life-threatening illness is: *Blessed art Thou, Our Lord, our God, King of the universe, Who has given you to us, and has not given you to the dust.* As for old age, there's the beautiful plea of David in Psalm 71: *Do not cut me off in the time of old age; do not forsake me when my strength fails.* But as far as I could tell, there were no blessings specifically tailored to those, like my maternal grandmother, whose bodies outlast their minds.

My beautiful, highly spirited, brilliant grandmother—the Nana who had taken me to Scandinavia when I was eighteen, introduced me to sushi, bought tickets for Broadway plays, and told me stories about her girlhood in Henderson, Kentucky—was now a crone in a bed, her memory banks all but wiped out by a series of small strokes that had left her at first merely bewildered and then increasingly panicked, anxious, and vulnerable. All those stories she'd told me, all her personal history, had vanished for her, and she now lived in an unending present tense. One day, a few years earlier, she'd gone out for a quart of milk and looked up to realize that she didn't know where she was. She wandered up and down Lexington Avenue for a while, until a kindly stranger returned her to her own building, some blocks away, on East 68th Street. She bought gallons of vitamins, dozens of magazine subscriptions, and strings of fake pearls. Her toenails became infected with fungus; her gums bled. Stains the size and shape of Rorschach inkblots began to appear in her bathrooms and the house she'd always kept with such Victorian stridency fell into musty, dusty decay. Then her jewelry and silver disappeared, along with her housekeeper, and that, finally, was enough. She was then in her mid-eighties. My mother and her sister sold the apartment in New York and the house in "the country" and moved her, first, into an old age home in Connecticut, where my aunt, who lived in Scarsdale, could look after her, and then—when my aunt ran off with her high school boyfriend (divorcing her first husband of forty-six years and sending Scarsdale into tizzies of gossip)—into a single room in an Alzheimer's facility in Chevy Chase, Maryland.

My mother had a brother, too, my uncle. Because my uncle lived on the West Coast, I never really knew him the way I knew my other aunts and uncles. And also, there was this: somewhere along the line, he became a born-again Christian. He wore a little cross in his lapel and talked about how he could both be Jewish and worship Jesus as his personal savior. My father could barely tolerate him when he was in this mode. "The White-hills," he'd say, rolling his eyes. "With the exception of your mother, the whole damn family is completely nuts."

Right now all I knew was that my mother had asked me to keep Nana's memories for her. The only problem was, you can't keep another person's memories. I could barely make sense of my own. But Mom insisted, adding that, by virtue of my having moved South, I'd somehow recaptured, or was in the act of recapturing, Nana's life. "That close-knit Jewish community, it's just like what Mother had," she'd say. But Mom got it backward: Nana had left the South as a young woman in search of grander vistas and a bigger stage and never dreamed of returning, whereas Stuart and I had come South because Stuart was born to be a law professor and LSU offered him a job. My grandmother had grown up in the small town of Henderson, in western Kentucky, just across the river from Evansville, Indiana—a place defined, at least how I envisioned it, as much by its Midwestern sensibility as by its Southern one—whereas we were living in a sprawling, post-Interstate overgrown state capital characterized more by its endless housing developments and staggeringly large numbers of fast-food outlets than by its discrete, old, riverfront downtown. I'd never so much as set foot in Kentucky, let alone visited the shrine that was my grandmother's hometown. Her ancestors, I supposed, were buried there, but as for living relatives—my mother's maternal aunt and uncle, as well as their children and grandchildren—they had scattered, and as a child I was barely aware of their existence at all.

I hadn't dipped into the Memory Books for years, and now I saw an entire world long gone—a sweeter world, I think, than ours—of small-town America, of sporting events and socials, before television turned the nations' minds to goop, and before the 1927 Mississippi flood came and washed out a great swath of the middle part of the country. I became nostalgic for a time and place I'd never known and felt my blood rush through my veins, as if I were recalling some long-forgotten memory of my own, or experiencing déjà vu. Nana's familiar round handwriting scrawled over the pages: *Gorgeous game! I played my best and made a goal from the center of the floor. (I have been captain in all our games.) Easy game and perfectly wonderful people! Marvelous time. Do I remember Charles Armstrong? I Say I Do!!!!*

Absolutely a "High" club. Members are seven girls, namely Juicy, Judy, Katherine, Elizabeth L., Carfie, Sue, and me. We have wonderful times hiking, going to all the shows together, and giving dances. Of course we send telegrams to "THE" team when it is out of town and we work for the athletic association on everythin'. We've got the spirit "that gets 'em" and plenty of PIP—Altogether now!!

There are also hundreds of newspaper clippings, invitations, dance cards, letters, corsages, theater programs, rings, cigarette butts, ticket stubs from high school sporting events, school compositions, ribbons, Christmas cards, progress reports, bottle caps, letters, postcards, photographs, menus, and telegrams. What emerged before me was a young, fearless girl in the midst of making herself. Even the death of her father, in 1919, didn't mar her sense of possibility, of all those worlds beyond Henderson that she glimpsed, every summer, when she went on the "circuit" throughout small towns in the South, to stay with relatives and meet other Jewish boys and girls. Their photographs are here, too—fresh-faced kids mugging for the camera, the boys in suits and ties, the girls with their bobbed hair. Most of them are long gone.

What was this urge of hers, I wondered, to record every moment, to save every document and memento of her youth? Did she know, even then, that it would vanish, not just from the world but from her mind?

Landing in the Port of New Orleans just before the outbreak of the Civil War, my mother's German-speaking forebears made their way overland to the mid-South, where they underwent a rapid population explosion, becoming, in a generation or two, a family of small-town shop-owners, lawyers, bankers, and brokers. Nana's father, Leon, was a typical representative of this class of Southern Jewish shop-owners, with his hardware and tack shop, Leon Levy and Sons, just off Main Street in Henderson, Kentucky. As a child, my grandmother liked to walk from her house on South Main to her father's store and hide among the barrels of oats and stacks of twine and rope.

I knew about the hardware store, and I knew about Henderson, because Nana told stories. She told lots of stories. She told stories about the hardware store and also told stories about collecting Indian arrowheads on the banks of the Ohio River and about going to dances and tea parties and minstrel shows and football games, and about winning the 1923 Western Kentucky Oratorical Contest with a paper entitled "The Present Unrest," beating out a boy named Wayne Priest. She also told me about the day her father Leon was killed, his spleen punctured, in his brand-new Model T Ford, and about how, a few days after he'd been buried, her mother came to her, saying, "Baby Jennie, you must take charge now" and handing over the household keys. She told stories about her cousins in St. Louis, Missouri, and in Monroe, Louisiana, and all the parties and dances she went to, and all the football games Barrett Manual Training High School won: "Why, the boys were simply divine, we all were!" There were stories about her two grandmothers, whom she referred to all her days as "Henderson Grandma" and "Jackson Grandma," and about taking the train to Baltimore, in 1919, when she was a sixteen-year-old freshman at Goucher College. And then she told stories about my grandfather, Clarence—who died shortly before I was born—but not many of them, because I think when my grandfather died, all the real fun went out of Nana's life. My grandfather was a New Yorker, and Nana's personal mythology—as little Jennie Esther Levy from Henderson, Kentucky, who grew up to be the charming Mrs. Clarence Whitehill of Scarsdale and Sutton Place—took root.

Even in her eighties, when Stuart, who was then my boyfriend, first met her, Nana was so immensely charming that I could see him sort of melting, changing shape as he sat opposite her in her living room, sipping Lillet from a small, cut-crystal aperitif glass. Chatting about Proust and Picasso, the plight of Palestinians in Israel and Jews in the Soviet Union, my grandmother was dressed simply in a pink silk blouse and gray wool skirt, her gray hair swept back over her high forehead, a diamond-encrusted wedding band on her ring finger. She sat on a chintz-covered settee, nodding intently each time Stuart made an observation or offered a theory of his own, drawing him out as discreetly as an old courtesan would. In the fireplace was a fire, on the sideboard a vase filled with freesia, on the opposite wall were a Picasso, a Rauschenberg, and two prints by Marc Chagall, and over the sofa hung a large portrait of my grandmother at thirty or so, posed formally, dressed in an elegant gown, her hair piled on top of her head: a great, if somewhat haughty beauty, the pride in her stance and expression softened only by some sadness that you sensed but could not name. Stuart gazed at it, and then at my grandmother, and then back at the portrait.

She told him one of my favorite stories: in 1928, when Nana was herself a young mother in New York, her cousin Dorothy Freeman was an undergraduate at a women's college in Virginia. During Christmas vacation, when Dorothy was home in Henderson, she told her daddy that there'd been some robberies on campus and asked if she could take his shotgun for protection. "The very day she returned to college," Nana continued, wide-eyed, while my new boyfriend sat mesmerized, "she shot herself." Stuart gasped. "Poor Aunt Hattie was never the same," my grandmother concluded, with a little shiver, a frisson, of resigned despair. "Never."

Luis Buñuel said: "Life without memory is no life at all. . . . Our memory is our coherence, our reason, our feeling . . . without it we are nothing." Had my grandmother, a victim of her own misfiring synapses, been reduced to nothing before our eyes? Had her soul been robbed from her? And if so, where was she—where was her soul—now?

The late Rabbi Aryeh Kaplan put it this way: "We know that God is omniscient. He knows all and does not forget. God knows every thought and memory that exists in our brains. There is no piece of information that escapes His knowledge. What, then, happens when a man dies? God does not forget, and therefore all of this information continues to exist, at least in God's memory."

But Nana wasn't dead. She was simply no longer Nana.

Actually, Nana was hardly the first of her line to record every moment. Her mother, Celeste, kept copious records of Nana's infancy, noting every gift she was given at birth, every footstep, every milestone. Doubtless my own impulse to write everything down, to record it for keeps, is genetic. I come from a family of inveterate storytellers and amateur historians. One of Nana's cousins, Celeste Felsenthal, composed a family history, which was published in Memphis in 1928, but this, too, is a compilation of an earlier family history, written by another, older cousin in 1891. Nana entrusted her copy to me shortly before I was married. Here is a piece of it: *The first of our ancestors of whom I have any knowledge is a certain Isaac. He lived in the beginning of the eighteenth century, in the town of Idar, near Oberstein, on the Nahe River. His son was Jacob Isaac, born in 1732. He settled in the village of Rathskirchen, in the northern part of the present Bavarian Rheinpfalz, and died there in 1807. He left four sons and three daughters, viz., Isaac, Herz, Israel, Davele, Sarah, Miriam, and Yettele. In 1807, the family had adopted the surname of Felsenthal. This had to be done in accordance with a decree of the Emperor Napoleon, which required all Jews in France to adopt regular family names. Rheinpfalz, where the family then resided, was at that time a part of the French empire.*

What's so remarkable about this document is not only that I can trace my own ancestry back to the seventeenth century (the "a certain Isaac" in the passage above was Nana's great-great-great grandmother's great-great-great grandfather, making him my great-great-great-great-great-great-great grandfather), but also, simply, that I have it. It reminds me of the begats in Genesis 46. Most American Jews don't have anything like this cornucopia of family history at their fingertips, in part because when the Holocaust wiped everyone out, whole generations vanished, and along with them their family stories.

And all this was on my mind—though not in any coherent way—when, just a few weeks after she'd sent me the Memory Books, Mom called to say that Nana was in the hospital, suffering from a respiratory infection. My mother had long since expressed a wish that Nana die before she herself did, because, as she put it, "If I go first, who the hell will look after Nana? Your father?" My mother had always been very competitive. With her, everything was always "the best," or it didn't really count, an attitude that she'd inherited directly from Nana, who was so competitive that even after her brain cells went on strike, she could recount, in excruciating detail, the 1912 girls' basketball game against Owensboro, in which she'd scored the winning basket—well of course she had, she was *the best*. She made everybody else look like they had sand in their drawers. My mother and my grandmother were now in a race to the finish line, only, of course, in this case Mom wanted to lose. "Maybe we'll all get lucky and she'll die in her sleep," Mom said, but the next day she called me and said that Nana had gotten out of her bed in the hospital, padded down the hall, and ended up two stories down, eating lunch off someone else's lunch tray. When an orderly finally found her, she looked up at him, batted her eyelashes, and in her sweetest Southern accent, said, "You're simply darling to escort me home."

Nana hung on, but my paternal grandmother, Helene—we called her "Grandma"—didn't. She died a few months after Nana's adventure in the hospital, when she was just two months shy of her ninety-fourth birthday. In some ways, she was the lucky one. She died in her sleep, at home in Baltimore, her system weakened by a recent bout of pneumonia. But Grandma had inhabited her own personality until the last moments of her life. (She had lamb chops—her favorite—for dinner on the night she died.) When we went to visit her, it was the old Grandma, the grandmother I had always known, who kissed me hello and insisted that I eat a decent lunch. Moreover, she was always engaged, eager to hear about us, talk about the great events of the day, and learn our opinions of, say, the latest scandal coming out of Washington.

But she was also the unlucky one. Her eyesight began to go when she was in her late seventies. She was widowed around the same time. Her closest friends dropped off, one by one, until "the girls" who were her lifelong companions were all gone. Toward the end of her life, she was all but cut off from the world by her own failing body. She was legally blind, she had a hard time hearing, and she couldn't walk. She moved around her apartment in a motorized wheelchair, which she needed help getting in and out of. She needed help in the bathroom. She needed help at the dinner table. She needed help getting dressed. And all this time, she knew exactly what was happening to her. Her mind remained sharp even while her body fell apart.

Unlike Nana, Grandma didn't dip into her own biography: She didn't keep diaries, and in fact rarely spoke of herself at all, believing, I suppose, that her own private concerns were of no great interest. But not for a second did she forget who she was. Not for a moment did she grow confused about her own family history and that of her husband or have to be reminded of which photograph, of the dozens that adorned her shelves, corresponded with which great-grandchild. From the time she was married, she had taken on the burdens of my grandfather's huge, Orthodox family, both living and dead, and as far as I could tell, she did it willingly. There had never been a time when her living room hadn't been dominated by the portraits of my great-great grandparents—the genius hatmaker, founder of the family dynasty, and his pious, Orthodox, devoted wife. The portraits themselves are stunningly beautiful, with the figures of my great-great-grandparents emerging gracefully out of a dark brown gloom, their faces pearly and smooth, a quiet smile playing on my great-great-grandmother's lips, while beside her, my great-great grandfather looks into the half-distance with an expression of pure wistfulness that peaks from under an outer layer of something approaching wise certainty, as if he were trying to look stern but couldn't quite manage it. But when I was a child, the portraits simply freaked me out, and I often wondered why my grandmother, who otherwise seemed balanced, would be content to live with two such gloomy specters.

Accompanied by Sam, who was now eleven years old, I flew from Baton Rouge to Washington for the funeral. My father picked us up in his pickup truck (his version of a midlife-crisis car), and the next day Dad and I drove to Baltimore early so Dad could have a chance to say goodbye to his mother in private, before the inevitable press of friends and relatives. It was brutally hot outside, but inside the funeral home the temperature was hovering just above freezing. The place was so quiet—its floors covered with smooth carpeting, its walls thick, and its employees professionally silent—that I felt like I was breathing too loudly. The undertaker showed us into the private room—it was sort of like a large, walk-in closet—where my grandmother's body awaited burial, and left us there.

Judaism is pretty strict about burial and mourning rituals, instructing, for one thing, that coffins be cheap and simple and that the corpse itself return to the earth clothed in no more than a shroud. Nor is the corpse supposed to be gussied up for viewing, the idea being that dust is already returning to dust. But my grandmother was wearing a lovely, high-necked silk dress, of swirling blues and greens, and her hair was arranged—as if, even in death, she was asserting not only her individuality but also her fashion sense. The hell with German Jewish propriety. Grandma was going to God in style. My father opened the casket, said a brief prayer, and kissed her goodbye.

Later, during the memorial service, the officiating rabbi delivered a painfully long-winded and mind-numbing eulogy, filled with empty, flowery phrases. The theme of this sermon was that my grandmother was an *eshet hayal,* or valorous wife, that she was committed to Jewish values, and that she was kind to everyone she'd ever met—all of which was true, but somehow missed the point anyway. By the time the rabbi at last stepped down, some twenty or twenty-five minutes after he'd first taken the pulpit, I was ready to whack him over the head with a shovel.

Doubtless my grandmother Helene truly was—as the verbose rabbi had said over and over—an *eshet hayal,* but to me she wasn't emblematic of anything, not even of her own self. As a child, I had never felt very drawn to her, perhaps because she wasn't a very inviting person. I don't mean to imply that she was cold; it was more like she was somewhat vague, that she didn't really possess much of a personality at all, beside this kind of steely calm that radiated neither approval nor disapproval, disgust nor delight. She was the grandmother who sat at the end of the table during Thanksgiving and Passover and summoned the black help in the kitchen; who then served heaping dishes of chicken or turkey, various kinds of vegetables, spiced peaches (a favorite in my grandmother's house), soft dinner rolls, and at least two kinds of cakes for dessert. In the kitchen were the omnipresent Jessie and Hilda, with their slow, old-fashioned way of talking and their white uniforms; and in the next room, hanging on the wall behind two large leather-covered wingback chairs, were the portraits of my grandfather's grandparents. All of us knew where the moxie lay: with that amazing line of my grandfather's. It lay in my grandfather and my father, and eventually, it would be passed onto my brother, David. Surely the portraits would one day go to David, too, and Grandma would fade into nothingness. But as she climbed into great old age, my grandmother softened and ripened; she seemed indeed to be blooming; kindness and joy radiated from her face, and grace from her fingertips. And as for the portraits, they, too, changed. Now when I visited my grandmother in her apartment in Baltimore, my great-great grandparents seemed to gaze at me not with disapproval or disgust but with kind, even joyful, acceptance, as if they only wanted what was best for me and appreciated my attentions—however unheroic—to my frail, brave, ancient grandmother.

A few months after Grandma's funeral, my father called to tell me that he wanted me to have the portraits of my great-great-grandparents. "Because you'll treasure them," he said.

7

Glimpses

One Sufi proverb says: "Faith is verification by the heart; profession by the tongue; action by the limbs." I don't know about numbers One and Two, but I finally got number Three down pretty good. After I made my first painting, I couldn't stop; my hand wanted to hold a paintbrush as if it were the hand of God Himself. I was seeing visions, too: rabbis falling out of the sky, and people dancing, and eyes peering down from the sky as prayers flew up from the earth. The visions came to me fully formed, one after another, sometimes so furiously that I couldn't sleep but instead kept popping up to sketch out each vision—to take notes on it, as it were—before it fled into the night. Was this God, talking to me in images? At the time, I didn't think so. I thought that the paintings I was making were an expression of some part of the "real" me that had gotten lost along the way, that part of my soul that had gone underground during all my years of neurotic misery. Now I think otherwise.

But the way it was with Joanna was this: for her, Jesus was real, period, a living, breathing presence. I know, because one day I asked her point blank. We were in St. Anthony's small, over-air-conditioned kitchen, while in the living room a bunch of residents were nodding off to *Sally Jessy Raphael,* their T cells disappearing with each commercial break.

"You want to know how I know Jesus is *real*?" Joanna said.

Actually, I wanted her to tell me how I myself might meet Jesus: what I had to do, what attitude I might take, to meet Him up close and personal, only hold the Christianity, starting with the Personal Savior stuff. I wanted Joanna to tell me how—exactly—I might know the inner peace and freedom that she seemed to claim as her birthright. Couldn't she just give me the recipe? A little bit of prayer, some singing, perhaps a few good deeds, mix it all together, add some chocolate chips, and bake in the oven at 350—just substitute Adonai for Christ, and it's kosher: Voilà! God. Because, let's face it, at first glance, most people, if given a choice of whose life they'd rather inhabit, mine or Joanna's, would choose mine. Most people—or at least most people in my world—would rather be well-off and white, with vacations in Maine and trips to the islands, than distinctly not-well-off and black, with a small apartment in Livingston Parish, a low-paid job, and car payments from now until doomsday. But Joanna, as she told me in no uncertain terms, was rich. Inside, where her real life was lived, her spirit was huge, free, untroubled. There was so much Jesus in her, she said, that there were times when she couldn't keep Him inside anymore, when she had to sing His praises, when her apartment became a church, and she became the preacher, congregation, and choir.

Joanna told me that she'd always been a Christian, but not necessarily a *Christian* Christian, not a Christian in her heart. She said that though she'd been raised Christian, she hadn't always known Jesus. Not *really.* She hadn't even been much interested in him. He came to her anyway, one night when she was laid up in the bed, her back sore from lifting too many old people (she'd had a job working at an old-age home then), her mind sore from the pain of living, at a time in her life when she was all twisted up and feeling sorry for herself. She said that one night when she was just lying there, her heart a stone, her blood bitter, a friend called her to ask her: would she speak to this man? This man could help her. And Joanna thought: yeah, okay, why not? The next day, the man called her, saying that the Lord had instructed him to call her—and then he went on and told Joanna all kinds of things about herself, secret things, hidden things that no one else in the entire world knew about, like the bad dreams that had plagued her as a child, and the worries she had for her daughters. "He looked straight into my heart and knew what was inside it," Joanna said. "And when I asked him if he was playing a trick on me, he laughed and said that Jesus had given him a gift, and that Jesus was now telling him that my back hurt not because I was injured in my *back,* but because I was injured in my *heart.* My heart was closed to the Lord, and if I wanted to get better, I had to let the Lord in. He told me to get up and get dressed and to go to the Mount Zion Holy Baptist Gospel Church."

"Then what happened?"

"I went."

"And?"

"You really want to know?"

Want to know? I was hanging onto every word.

Because what happened next was even better. What happened next was that, one night when Joanna was sleeping, an apparition who she identified as Jesus himself flew in through the open window and stood in front of her, his legs braced apart, his arms open, so she could get a good, long look at him. She liked the looks of him well enough, but that wasn't what tipped her off, because he looked just like an ordinary man—about five feet ten or so, with close-cropped hair and slightly big ears, wearing a Southern Jaguars sweatshirt, jeans, and white tennis shoes—except that he was somewhat translucent, and he glowed. He had a white light coming off of him, but no wounds or scars or bloody palms—nothing at all, in fact, that made him look like he'd spent the past two thousand years or thereabouts hanging on a cross. He stood right there, just as easy as you please, kind of smiling a little, as if recollecting an especially funny joke, or a family picnic, or the first time he kissed a girl.

She looked at him, and he looked at her, and for a while they just looked at each other like that, but by the time he left, Joanna felt that she'd been transformed. The old Joanna, with all her ordinary aches and pains, was gone, and the new Joanna—the one who lived in the light—was born.

"That was Jesus," Joanna added, almost as an afterthought, "and I could hear him loud as day."

I asked her if she heard Jesus as a voice inside her head—as I myself hear my own best conscience—or if the voice sounded "real."

"Baby, I could hear Jesus' words as clearly as I hear you now. When Jesus is talking to me, he's *talking* to me," Joanna said, giving me a little grimace, as if to say: Is the sky blue? Is the Pope Catholic?

"What do you mean, you struggle with faith?" she'd say to me, over and over. "Only one thing you got to know: Jesus is real, baby. And he ain't never going to leave you."

When Stuart asked me that night over dinner how my day had been, I went ahead and told him all about how Jesus had paid Joanna a personal visit, and when I was done, Stuart said, "Fine, Jen, but she's crazy." Which, of course, was exactly what Stuart was going to say, because Stuart is rational. A few days later, at Beth Shalom, I told Rabbi Stan the same story. "I just don't know what to make of this," I said. "I mean: Angels? Apparitions in Southern Jaguars sweatshirts? And if Joanna gets angels and apparitions in Jaguars sweatshirts, why don't I?" I meant it, too. What am I, chopped liver? But Rabbi Stan merely sighed, glanced up at me, and said: "God speaks to each of us in a language we can understand."

8 |

Afterward

We'd been in Baton Rouge for six years when, a month or so before Passover, Stuart and I went to Tucson, Arizona, for the weekend, leaving our three children, ages eleven, seven, and seven, with a babysitter. We went because the University of Arizona law school was interested in hiring Stuart as a visiting professor, with the possibility of the position turning into a full-time one; and, on the theory that they wouldn't get the husband without the wife's approval, they invited both of us out to take a look around. They'd even lined up a realtor to give us a tour of the local housing market.

Stuart wanted the job, which turned out not to exist but at the time seemed to simultaneously represent a step up on the academic ladder and a better town—the kind of town that people on the East Coast might actually even want to visit—but my own feelings were decidedly more mixed. After all, I *liked* Baton Rouge. Within five minutes of breathing the desert air, though, I was convinced that Tucson was paradise. There are Democrats in Tucson—loads of them—and old idealistic hippies of every stripe. There are artists and dancers, coffee bars and independent bookstores, practitioners of Reiki and yoga centers on every corner. The air is clean, the hills are covered with wildflowers, people go around dressed in floppy, light-colored linens and sandals and eat fresh vegetables. St. Anthony's would get along without me. And as far as Beth Shalom went, who needed Beth Shalom? My bat mitzvah? I'd do it in the desert. In Tucson there were half a dozen synagogues to choose from, and one of them actually invited us to join them on Shabbat morning for worship services at the top of a canyon. The closest we ever got to nature at Beth Shalom was the parking lot. Come Saturday morning, Stuart and I, along with a dozen or so members of the Tucson synagogue, climbed past cacti and prickly pears, through ancient red rock embedded with the fossil remains of a thousand extinct undersea creatures. At last we arrived at a deep pool fed by a waterfall, where, on large flat rocks at water's edge, both men and women donned yarmulkes and prayer shawls, gathered in a circle, and began to chant the prayers: *Baruch Ata Adonai, Elohanu Melach ha-olam, sheasani Yisrael.* Blessed is the Eternal our Lord, who has made me a Jew. My voice, along with those of my fellow Jews, rose in the desert air, echoing off the cliffs and climbing to the heavens.

By the time, several hours later, the realtor whom the law school had lined up picked us up at our hotel, I was ready to pack my bags. "I think you'll be very pleased with the housing market," she said as we rounded the corner in her sleek, silver Mercedes. I didn't respond. I was too busy decorating our new house—the one with the white stucco walls, exposed beams, and tile floors—filling it with tribal rugs and big jugs of wildflowers, modern art, books. And there I was, on the terrace: I'm doing yoga, or perhaps I'm painting. I'm doing yoga *and* I'm painting, and my hair is pulled behind me, in a braid. How happy, how radiant, how peaceful I look. And that is because I have become Pure. I have achieved Godhead. I am glowing with light. All the crap, all the mess, of my normal, everyday life is a thing of the past: the irritating woman at Beth Shalom who always corners me after services to insist that I write a letter to the editor on whatever is bugging her at that moment, the nut-ball who rails against Bolshevism as if the Russians were about to invade Baton Rouge, the neighbor who likes to tell me that Clinton was the anti-Christ—all of them are gone, vanquished, dispensed with. Indeed, I am on a new, higher plane altogether, joyful, *actualized.* I am like a saint, or a guru, or even a prophet, but better looking, and a lot more stylish. We won't move to Tucson, but I don't know that yet, and so, as I sit in the front seat of the realtor's Mercedes, I am gazing at the foothills that surround our new, imaginary house, envisioning the herbs I'll grow in terra-cotta containers on the slate terrace, and writing with such great fluidity and charm that it's as if I were merely taking dictation. I'm enraptured by my new life. Then I hear Stuart scream.

"Look out!"

His voice is high-pitched, strained, weird, and just as his words register there is a terrible blow, a sickening crunch, and the car, as it swings around, seems filled with heat. Though none of it seems possible—this nauseating, dislocating terror, this rearranged landscape, the trees and fences sliding by sideways, the trash cans parading backward, the blue of the sky bouncing off the ochre tones of the earth—I know exactly what is happening. I've been preparing for it, in some sense, my whole life. It's what I've felt dozens of times when, in the worst of my nightmares, the car I'm riding in skids off the highway, or the airplane I'm in tumbles from the sky. It's what my friend Carrie, in Washington, had talked about, when she talked about the death, by cancer, of her father: *I felt good knowing that he knew where he was going, that he had time to prepare, and that he knew I was by his side.* It's what Bev did, when she closed her eyes and said, "Enough." It's what Mom talks about every time she calls me. Only what's happening to me isn't happening slowly. Prepare my soul to meet my maker? There's no time.

Sh'ma Yisrael: Adonai Elohanu, Adonai Echad. Hear O Israel: The Lord is God, the Lord is One. The same words that were on the lips of the martyrs as they were burned at the stake or gassed in Hitler's ovens, and now I'm saying them too. Over the roar of the impact, I can hear my voice inside my throat. *Sh'ma . . . Yisrael.* One at a time, the words coming out slowly. I'm not sure I'll have enough time to get to the end. My three children are going to be orphaned. I know this as surely as I know the sound of my mother's voice, or the feeling of hunger in my guts, or my own fatigue. I just know it. I know it in my bones. Why else would the words have sprung so readily to my lips?

The car lurches, a terrible, groaning sound, and I'm here in the passenger seat, helpless and completely alone. Where's my husband? In the back seat, a million miles away. A place I can't reach. The truth is, I'm not even thinking about him, not really, except in a vague way that has more to do with the children. Nor am I thinking about the driver—who at any rate is barely an acquaintance. Only she too has a life: a husband, children. What was *wrong* with her, anyway? Didn't she see that car barreling over the hill? No, she couldn't have. She was too busy pointing to the map, chattering on about the delights of Tucson real estate. Tucson? Who cares about Tucson? I'll never see Baton Rouge again; never see my children, and all because this frosted-blonde idiot wasn't paying attention to what she was doing. The children! The twins are in second grade, reading "chapter books." Rose is so beautiful she melts hearts. Jonathan never stops asking questions. Who will break the news to them? They'll barely remember us. They'll be raised by someone else. Who? Stuart and I had gone over and over this question just a few months ago, as we prepared to make our wills. My parents are too old, and, in any event, who knows how much longer Mom's health will hold? Binky is perennially, stubbornly single. My brother has four of his own. My little sister, Amalie, then? She lives in Vermont, where there are cows and snow. Stuart's brother? But he lives in Jerusalem—too far away, and surrounded by unfriendly nations. His sister? In the end we made a decision, but as we sat in our lawyer's office in Baton Rouge, I couldn't help but think that now that our wills were made, we may as well have been carrying a big sign that said, "Okay, God, we're ready to go!" But all this is in a jumble, a rush of indistinct thoughts that fly by in a moment, and in the end all I'm thinking about—though it's not exactly thinking—is my own little life, my precious and only life, about to be snuffed out. Painfully. And what about my mother? Hasn't she had enough misery? I don't think she can endure this. And was it last week or the week before that I heard Joanna at St. Anthony's telling a new resident: "Call out to the Father, child, He already know what's in your heart before you even tell Him, but you got to tell Him anyway, child, don't you know He love you?"

But I don't have time to call out to God, my human father is far away, my mother still has a tumor inside her, Nana is only half alive, and I'm going to die.

But my mother and grandmother get pushed out, too, in this terrible careening as the car spins around, the impact of the metal shooting straight up my spine, the world tilting dangerously but not unfamiliarly—it's every bad dream and every tense movie I've ever seen, it's *ER*, *NYPD Blue*, and the Roadrunner all running together like scrambled eggs. Only this time I know the ending: Stuart and I crushed by a car. What will we tell our kids? Oops: someone else will have to tell them, someone else will have to wipe their tears. Only yesterday we'd assured them that we'd be back home before they knew it. Please, dear God, take care of my children.

I'd wept with joy when Sam arrived. We named him Samuel, the same name that Hannah chose for the only son whom she'd prayed for at the Shrine of Shiloh with such fervor that, though she didn't speak, her lips moved. So intent was Hannah on her prayer that the priest, Eli, thought she was a drunkard and ordered her to leave. Instead she explained that she was a servant of the Lord, and pledged her child to God's service. The priest blessed her, and nine months later she gave birth to a baby boy, whom she named Shmuel: God hears.

God? Can You hear me? Are You there?

Rose and Jonathan came more painfully, after a labor that seemed to go on for forever, and a difficult pregnancy. The night before they were born, my doctor had assured me that the boy (we knew that I was carrying one of each) was in the head-down position at the top of the birth canal, ready to be born. He told me to get a good night's sleep, but all night long, I felt as if there was a dance party in my womb: *boom boom chick-a-boom*—the return of disco! And the next day, it wasn't Jonathan, but his sister, Rose, who emerged first, all pink and round, with long, black eyelashes. Jonathan came twenty minutes later, looking a bit beat-up, a bit worn-out, from what we now knew was a night-long wrestling contest with his twin sister. He opened his eyes, blinked twice, and, as if to say, "Catch you later," closed them again. Would anyone know this story after I was gone? Would the twins know how desperately we'd wanted them, how delighted we were in them, how we'd stand over the crib they shared during their first months, looking first at one and then the other, saying, "one baby, two babies." Who will remember my memories for me?

Sh'ma Yisrael Adonai Elohanu Adonai Echad.

Then the car comes to a stop. Just like that the engine hisses, steam rising from it. Every part of me is here: my fingernails, my knees, the rubber band at the end of my braid. In the back seat, Stuart is breathing with difficulty, but a minute later I can hear him saying, "I can't see a damn thing. Where are my glasses?" The world—the whole solid *thingness* of it, its raggedness, its impossibility—comes rushing back. Trees and sidewalks. The smell of burning rubber. Sweat in my armpits and an urgent need to empty my bladder and a staleness in my mouth and the sound of an approaching siren and of people running toward us, yelling. "Are you all right? Is anyone hurt?" We unlatch our seatbelts and walk slowly to the sidewalk.

It didn't take long to figure out what had happened. A black SUV, its front end now smashed in, had been racing another SUV on the other side of a slight rise as two lanes merged into one, just as our realtor had been nudging the Mercedes forward across the intersection. (In other words, some asshole had to prove what a big dick he had.) But what was harder to figure out was *why*. Not why we'd had the accident, but why we were still alive.

To this day I'll never know how close we actually came to death, or even if such a calculation is possible. All I know is that I *knew* my time was up, and then it wasn't. At the time, all I could do was cry, crying and crying as if crying were the natural expression of my soul, the only way I could communicate. Relief came flooding in the moment I knew that Stuart was okay, but the shock of the instant, the sheer terror, followed by the enormous sense of having escaped my own grave—that clung to me. And though I soon found my tongue and began to talk, and talk and talk and talk and talk, all the words that streamed out of my mouth seemed as meaningless and random as dust. I felt as though I was trying to describe a dream in Kiswahili or dig to China with a spoon.

Stuart pointed out that we didn't die—and indeed were barely hurt—because of a confluence of fortunate circumstances. We were wearing our seat belts; there was no oncoming traffic; the SUV hit behind the driver's seat, which was the only seat in the car where no one was sitting; and finally, we were in a Mercedes, built, he said, "like a tank." But he's a professional scholar, a person who'd gone to law school and, as an undergraduate, studied philosophy—a bona fide intellectual, with a truly neck-up style of cognition, complete with a reliance on rationality and reason. As far as I was concerned, the circumstances were only the circumstances: I wanted to know what the circumstances *meant*.

Years later, when we were again living in Baton Rouge after a yearlong sabbatical in Glasgow, Scotland, I started seeing a nun, Sister Dulce Maria, for spiritual counseling, which might seem odd for a Jew, but there you have it. And anyway, Sister Dulce isn't your ordinary nun, but a healing nun, who, like Rabbi Stan, believes that God is bigger than religion, and told me that even when I died, and went to heaven, I'd be Jewish. She also told me that, when she was a child of no more than five, she had almost drowned in the Gulf of Mexico, but just before she was about to lose consciousness, she heard a voice. The voice, she said, told her to bob to the surface and then to walk. "Breathe, walk, breathe, step forward," the voice said, and in that way, she was led up and out of the water. Had Sister Dulce told me this story before my own experience with the fragility of my own life, the utter vulnerability of my continuing existence, I'm not sure I would have believed her—or at the very least, I would have chalked her story up to some other, paranormal, extra-psychological force. But not a voice. Now I know better. Now I know that the voice that Sister Dulce heard was a direct manifestation of the voice of God, because God had no intention of letting the future Sister Dulce die.

Had God saved us, too? Had He spread out His hand and, as my daughter, Rose, later described it, pulled us from the wreck? And what really happened to us, after all? A terrifying four or five seconds, followed by some stiffness in our lower backs, a slight soreness in our rib cages. Big deal. We were lucky, poster children for a new Mercedes ad campaign featuring folks who've walked away from bad collisions. But when, back at our hotel, Stuart left the bedroom to take a bath, I was six years old again: on my knees, and from there down on the floor, in the posture of full supplication, thanking God for delivering us from death. Even while I was praying, however, I was self-conscious, filled with doubt, for, as Stuart and I have discussed many times since, any God who saves two middle-aged yuppies but allows countless innocent millions to suffer excruciating and horrible deaths and additional millions to endure deprivations that I can't even imagine is no God worth worshiping. But I continued to pray anyway. What else could I do?

In 1972, when my mother was exactly my age, she was driving home from a lunch date in McLean when a plumber's van ran through a stop sign and broadsided her station wagon. My mother's car was totaled—a heap of bent and fractured metal around her. Mom got a bad cut on her forehead and had to have stitches. The police said that the impact was so great that she should have been killed. At the time I didn't think too much about it, but at some point after I was out of college, she told me that she'd come within inches, and seconds, of losing her life. She had a faint scar, snaking up from the top of her forehead and disappearing into her hairline. Sometimes she touched it, as if to remind herself that she was still there.

The Shabbat liturgy includes the words of the Psalmist: How manifold are Your works, o Lord! The heavens declare Your glory!

Except that half the time, I'm too distracted, or too tired, or simply too bored—waiting in an endless line of Chevy Suburbans to pick up the twins from school or sitting in the dentist's office, flipping through the pages of *People* magazine while Sam gets his teeth capped, again, repairing the damage done when he decided to catch a baseball with his mouth—to see the glory of anything beyond the glass of red wine I let myself have every night.

As we flew east over the mountains, I tried to imprint what had happened to us into my brain cells, such that I might hold onto it, memorize it, impress the sound of the initial impact and the constriction of my throat into my hard drive. In his *Mishneh Torah,* the medieval Jewish philosopher Maimonides writes that the cry of the shofar on the Holy Days of Rosh Hashanah and Yom Kippur is "an allusion, as if to say, Awake, O you sleepers, awake from your sleep! O you slumberers, awake from your slumber! Search your deeds and turn in *teshuva.*"

I love that: *awake from your slumber!* And it's what I was thinking about, vaguely, as our airplane soared past the mountains and the foothills and at last over the endless brown flats of West Texas. I didn't want to go back to the way I was before. I didn't want to return to being psychically comfortable but spiritually dull, at ease in the world but only half awake, drifting through it in an overfed, air-conditioned, semi-stupor. Nor did I want to return to my old, fussy, petty self: the woman who freaks out over rejection slips from literary magazines on the one hand and stacks of dirty dishes on the other, who yells at her kids to quiet down already, she's going deaf, and what's more, can't you just go outside and play or something, or go somewhere, *anywhere*, where I can't hear you?

After my mother swam up from the misery of her first bout with chemotherapy and began to live her life again, she told me that all the unimportant things—the things that had formerly bothered her, like fat globs of toothpaste on the sink, or mold growing at the back of the vege-table drawer, or the fact that my father, after more than forty years of mar-riage, still couldn't manage to take his muddy boots off before he came into the kitchen after working outside in the garden—simply fell away. Maybe now, I thought, I'd be more like that. Maybe I'd stop obsessing about my weight and going around the house dust-busting every last piece of fuzz, sock-matter, and hairball. Maybe, I thought as we pulled into our driveway back in Baton Rouge, I'd finally learn to live in the moment, cherish human love, *chill out.*

"Try not to think about the accident too much," Stuart said as we headed up the stairs to our bedroom. "And don't talk about it in front of the children." But even as I tossed dirty clothes into the washing machine and put the two dresses I'd packed back in my closet, the questions bubbled up from my brain.

The rabbis say: *Keep two messages in your pocket. One: the world was made for me. Two: I am dust and ashes.* But already I could feel the memory of the accident slipping away; already I was making jokes about trading in my minivan for a Mercedes, snapping at the kids because they forgot to wipe their feet on the front mat, and fixating on how much I hated the rust-colored, vaguely Republican-looking curtains in our playroom.

At the time that he was arrested by the NKVD (the precursor of the KBG) in his cottage in Peredilkino and his manuscripts confiscated, the writer Isaac Babel was world famous. But under torture, Babel confessed to associating with Trotskyites, and in 1940, on Stalin's orders, he was shot. Babel went to his death mourning all the work he would never complete. But I had been saved. Why? And for what? I was proud of my little book, but it wasn't exactly *Tales of Odessa* or *Red Cavalry.* For my next one, then, the absolutely wretched *How's Bayou?*

By the time I knocked on Rabbi Stan's door a few days later, the memory—the physical memory, that is—was all but gone. I told him about what happened in Tucson, and my sense of having been saved, my counter-sense of having merely been lucky, and about how I was driving Stuart straight up the wall with my incessant, unanswerable questions. When I was done, Stan told me to come to Shabbat services. He said he'd do a special blessing designed for just such instances—the safe return home from a hazardous trip—in which the supplicant thanks God for deliverance from danger. I imagined a great release—a kind of flash-of-lightning, praise-the-Lord flood of emotion and love. At last I was going to be like the Christian faithful of Baton Rouge, those people so filled with the spirit of the Lord that they danced in the aisles, and, like King David, blessed His Holy Name with every limb, or like the Hasidim of Brooklyn, who danced ecstatically in the streets in celebration of God's having given Torah to the world.

But when Shabbat came two days later and I ascended the bimah to recite the blessing, rather than feel some rush of divine love or spark of knowledge or even some emotional release, mainly all I did was struggle with the unfamiliar Hebrew, choked with self-consciousness. *Praised are You, Lord our God, King of the Universe who graciously bestows favor upon the undeserving, even as He has bestowed favor upon me.* I could hear my mistakes and felt incredibly, horribly, publicly, and massively stupid. How could I possibly stand up before the congregation, not to mention my family, and read from Torah, when I couldn't even read a simple prayer of gratitude? How could I proclaim the grandeur of God and the beauty of the Sabbath day when, even now, I didn't know what to believe?

Amazing grace, how sweet the sound—

I wanted to remember those seconds of terror, the ache in my heart, the dread in my bones—and the miraculous moment when the car stopped and the world was restored to me—but I couldn't. All I could remember was the memory of the memory.

9|

Kaddish

Now that I had had my own brush with death, I thought that perhaps I'd feel a stronger connection to the residents of St. Anthony's. But the opposite was true. New people had moved in, none of whom was exactly a role model for anything other than self-destruction. There was Mitchell, handsome and friendly, as dark as ebony, who started hanging out with Gary, an ex-hairdresser, ex-husband, and ex-junkie who loved to buy tchotchkes at garage sales, and who made a point of mothering the more decrepit of his fellow residents, clucking and fussing over them like an old maw-maw. But one day I came to St. Anthony's and they, along with a third resident, Danny, were gone—because they'd been doing drugs in the bathroom. A few months later, Gary died, alone, at Earl K. Long. Then Mitchell died of a drug overdose. Three young women moved in, each of them the mother of several children, moved out again, moved in again, and died within weeks of each other. A middle-aged woman whose husband had infected her moved in, moved out again, and died. Then Valerie died. This is how I learned of her death: Caroline called me one morning and said, "The queen has died." I cried like a baby.

But I wasn't crying over Valerie alone. Valerie had been visibly failing for months, suffering cramps, gas pains, diarrhea, and utter immobility. She weighed about two hundred and eighty pounds; her legs were the size of telephone poles; tubes carried her pee to a plastic pouch suspended by the side of the bed. She'd long since lost both her eyesight and her ability to make some kind of coherent sense out of the swirl around her, in the process losing both her personal narrative, her personal *story*, and her grip on what most of us call reality. Her one daughter never came to visit her. Nor did her parents or any other family. I don't know why. Perhaps they were too embroiled in their own problems to so much as find the will to visit her. Perhaps they were scared by AIDS, by the prospect that they, too, might succumb to it—or perhaps they'd merely written her off, as early as four years earlier, when Valerie had first come to St. Anthony's. But she never did lose her sweetness, her hope, her sense of love and even enchantment with the world, and this is something I'm not sure I'll ever be able to understand. She missed her mamma, she said. She needed to see her, and did I know that her mamma was going to take care of her now that she was moving out of St. Anthony's, she was going home? She'd lie in her bed, the stories—or rather, the fragments of stories—just flying out of her mouth, her eyes rolling back in her head, while I held her hand, or the caregivers gave her a sponge bath or did her hair or told her to put her trust in God.

"Baby, that you, Jennifer? Jennifer, how about you spend the night with me?"

"Where would I sleep, Val?"

"Up here, in the bed with me."

"I don't think there's room for both of us."

"You take the chair, then."

"What would my husband say?"

"You tell him that he can sleep here too. You two do much nooky?"

"What?"

"He a good-looking man?"

Every time I left her bedside—either to go home or to hang out with another resident, I felt guilty. Joanna always told me not to feel guilty, that guilt was a wasted emotion, and that in any event, I did enough. But I didn't do enough, not really. And then another new resident, William, moved in, setting himself up in the room that, once upon a time, had been Gerald's, and I'd go and sit with him, sometimes for an hour, sometimes longer. William was easy to talk to, better educated than most of the other residents, and thoughtful. In his late sixties, William had a huge, bloated stomach, and stick-thin legs elevated on pillows in an effort to ease the swelling around his joints. He wore glasses and spent most of his days propped up on his neatly made bed, his room spotless, reading the Bible. He spoke in exact, almost persnickety sentences, drawing out the words to make a point, pausing over particularly complex ideas, and peppering his conversation with bureaucratic jargon, no doubt a holdover from his days working as some kind of mid-level manager in the Washington, D.C., city government. Proud of his education—he was a college graduate—and his articulate, refined speaking style, he told me stories about Washington under the first black mayor and during the civil rights and antiwar marches, a time that coincided with my own childhood in McLean. Sure beat hanging out with Val and trying to decipher her endless stream-of-consciousness, the gibberish that flew through her synapses and out her mouth in words that, more often than not, I couldn't understand. I wasn't the only one drawn to William, either. The visiting nurses who came to St. Anthony's, the janitorial staff, and the caregivers all doted on him. At times he seemed like the embodiment of a wise old man. But William's past was anything but inspirational. In fact, he was a murderer, and an unrepentant one. I know because, one day when I was sitting there shooting the breeze with him, just sitting back in the orange-colored fake-leather upholstered chair that St. Anthony's provides in all its rooms for visitors, laughing and nodding my head, he told me what he'd done up in Washington, D.C., before he took sick. He told me that he had had this quarrel with this man, and the man wouldn't see reason, so he had to shoot him, only it was the man's fault, and no, he didn't like to talk about the time he'd put in in the penitentiary in Virginia; those were long hard years, but he did his time, and it wasn't his fault anyhow, seeing how the man he'd shot and killed had it coming to him.

William had a dream: his dream was to return to Washington, where he'd been born and raised, and where he'd lived until recently, ending up in Baton Rouge, where he had a grandchild who was willing to look after him; only because he was sick and broke had he moved to St. Anthony's. He had money in the bank, he said, and just as soon as his legs felt better, just as soon as some of the swelling eased, why, he was going to get his money and go back to Washington.

And that's just what he did. He purchased a one-way ticket out of New Orleans and flew into Washington Reagan. He died at home the following week.

Then Valerie spiked a fever and was carted out to Summit Hospital, on the eastern edge of the parish. Shortly before she died, I went and visited her there. She lay alone in a private room, on oxygen. Her hair was a greasy mess; her eyes and eyelashes were coated with gunk; the corners of her beautiful lush lips were encrusted with dried saliva. Her fever, apparently, had come down, but any fool could see that she wasn't long for the world. I sat with her for a little while, fixing her hair and washing her face and hands, and then I kissed her goodbye. On my way out, I went to the nurses' station and explained that Valerie was special, that she was loved and loving, and could she—the nurse on duty—look in on her every now and then? Because after all, it wasn't as if Valerie were going to be using the phone or the call button. She didn't even know where she was. As I was driving home I made a mental note to call Miss Dolly and tell her that Valerie needed to be moved back to St. Anthony's, thinking that, at the very least, Valerie should die among people who loved her. But I never made the call. I got caught up in my kids' homework or soccer schedules, my own deadlines, dinner, e-mail, bills. Valerie died the next day. So when Caroline called me to tell me that the queen had died, my tears were for Valerie, but they were also for myself, for my good intentions that never turned to action.

Judaism has very strict, exacting rituals involving death and mourning. The body itself is prepared with utmost care, washed, and then placed in a shroud. Embalming is not permitted. Nor is any kind of makeup or hairstyle, which is seen as an insult both to the life that once inhabited the corpse and to the Maker of both life and death. The casket must be made of wood, and exceedingly simple—no satin lining, no inscriptions, no lettering, no gold. Barring extraordinary circumstances—such as flood or war—burial itself must take place within a day or two. Before burial, the community takes turns sitting with the deceased, reading Psalms aloud, and letting the family attend to more pressing concerns. This is done in accordance with the idea of the sacredness of human life, a sacredness that doesn't end in the body's death. I myself have acted as a member of Beth Shalom's informal *chevra kedusha*, or burial society, sitting with the dead for a two-hour shift until someone else comes to take my place. The idea is that the soul is not released to go to God until the body is buried; therefore, the body is kept company by other Jews, who keep watch all day and all night. This is a practice that has fallen into disuse in recent years, but the commandment to honor the dead is so central to Jewish communal life that the earliest synagogues in the South grew out of burial societies. When I first heard of this ancient custom, which is rooted in biblical times, it struck me as being rather silly. After all, the dead person is *dead*. They don't need your company. But Judaism doesn't see it that way: Judaism wants to prevent the dead person from feeling alone and believes that the first few hours after you die are especially tough for the soul, which has to get used to its new status and ready itself for its next phase.

The thirteenth-century Spanish sage Nachmanides, in his *Torah ha Adam*, or Law of Man, explicates the Jewish position on death in mourning in great detail. "Therefore," he wrote, "if a man dies earlier than most people die, of if a man's child dies, it is fitting that he, and those who love him, grieve and mourn—but their mourning must be such that it is a service of the Lord."

The beginning of the mourner's kaddish is:

> Magnified and sanctified
> May His Great Name be
> In the world that He created
> As He wills,
> And may His Kingdom come
> In your lives and in your days
> And in the lives of all the house of Israel
> Swiftly and soon,
> And let us say: Amen!

Dear God, I prayed after Valerie's death. *Let me walk the path that You desire for me. Let me do the work that You intend for me.* Because there was one thing I learned during all this: if you pray, you have to do it honestly. You have to tell God exactly what you mean, even if what you have to say isn't very nice. For example, I frequently pray for our government, but along the lines of: *Dear God in Heaven, in Your Infinite Knowing You know that I think George W. Bush is an incompetent nincompoop who ought to be taken out and tar and feathered, but Adonai, Elohanu, my God and God of my mothers and fathers, he's the only one we have, so please help us out a little, and replace some of that sausage he has between his ears with functioning gray matter.* I'm making jokes, but I mean it. Even if you don't believe in God, you have to pray, and moreover, you have to do it honestly. Because one thing I do know is that you can't bullshit God. Not that he'd mind, particularly, being used to it and all. It's more like you're just wasting time, spinning your own wheels, and let's face it, life's too short.

Let Thy will be done.

But what if His will is for me to stop writing and painting and playing the piano and doing yoga, so that I might serve the poor instead? Am I really prepared to hear the Voice of God, as Joanna had? Do I really want to know what He has in mind for me?

10

Coming of Age in Baton Rouge

Years ago, when we were still living in Washington and my mother gave every appearance of being on the brink of the grave, I spent more than a year and almost ten thousand dollars in therapy trying to get a handle on what my therapist—a lovely man who wore his hair hippie-style, in a little ponytail, and whose consulting room was a comforting jumble of tribal rugs, modernist prints, monographs, and books—said was the most unyielding case of denial that he'd ever seen. My mother was in and out of hospital rooms the way movie stars are in and out of rehab, first with one chemotherapy-induced infection, and then with another, and so on, until eventually I got to know my way around oncology wards all over town. After each visit I had to my mother's bedside, I brought back some new, unfunny quip. Her skin was the color of moldy newspaper, and I'd tell my therapist that she desperately needed to go to Elizabeth Arden for a facial. She was so skinny that she looked like she'd just been liberated from a concentration camp, and I'd say, "I guess she finally found a diet that works." She had no hair, and lay under blankets, shivering, her throat constricted, her mouth dry. "For the first time ever, I can get a word in edgewise," I'd say. All around me, sunshine-drenched dust motes danced. "It's better to face the truth now than later," my therapist would say, adding: "Later is too late." Made sense. But my heart, it seemed, was made of stone. Both my sisters would call me up on occasion, talk about Mom, and cry, but I felt nothing. And so I talked, and talked and talked and talked, about my complicated, tangled, frustrating relationship with my mother, starting back from the time when I was three and my mother threw out my beloved stuffed bunny rabbit, Bum Bum, and replaced her with a brand-new rabbit whose ears, enhanced by interior wires, stuck straight up (who did she think she was kidding?); and then moving up through my grade school ulcer; and then summer camp, where I was the camp loser, only Mom herself had gone to that same summer camp and therefore didn't understand that I couldn't hit a field-hockey ball if it were the size of Jupiter, and as for catching a softball, you may as well have asked me to grow wings and fly to Paris. I talked about not being sufficiently like my mother and her side of the family and about not being sufficiently like my father and his side of the family, either. I talked about camp again: all those athletic girls from rich old German Jewish families, all of whom, it seemed, had their periods at some reasonable time, whereas mine came late; and why had my mother sent me there in the first place? And what about my father? Why hadn't he rescued me? For that matter, how come neither one of them noticed that I was sliding into a depression so deep and so wide and so viscous that I felt like I belonged nowhere and to no one? And on and on I went, describing in detail every last misunderstanding, misalignment, and misjudgment that I'd endured in the course of what was in fact an extraordinarily privileged upbringing, wherein I was raised by a kind and good father who did his best, and a mother who, despite occasional lapses, loved me so desperately that, more often than not, I couldn't imagine a more perfect or sustaining love, or life without its author.

"And now your mother is dying," my therapist would say. "How do you feel about that?"

How did I feel about that? I felt lousy. Life without Mom? That would be bad. And how about the prospect of dealing with my father without Mom in her rightful place by his side, acting as a buffer zone? The very idea sent waves of panic fanning out along my collar bone. And what if Dad remarried? Yuck. On the other hand, I had other things to worry about, such as the fact that, at the time, I had one-year-old twins, a hyperactive four-year-old, and a career that seemed to be nothing more than a grandiose fantasy. Not to mention that we were about to leave civilization as I had always known it, for the dubious pleasures of what my husband was touting as a simpler, more authentically lived life in Baton Rouge. In the meantime, when she was feeling up to it, Mom initiated her practice of calling me on the phone to tell me exactly what kind of funeral she wanted, down to the flowers on her casket.

"Well?" my therapist said.

"God will not let my mother die," I said, "because He knows that the minute she dies, my father will marry some underage shiksa, and I will have a nervous breakdown for real."

"You're doing it again," my therapist said.

Finally, during one particularly difficult session, I managed to produce a rather impressive amount of tears, which seemed to convince my therapist—who was otherwise an amazingly insightful picker-upper of bullshit—that I had finally accepted the enormity of my imminent loss. But I hadn't. My heart was a fist. Other than the free-floating anxiety that I had experienced for most of my life, I was numb. And shortly thereafter, my husband and I packed up our stuff and moved away. When I kissed my mother goodbye, she sobbed until her entire emaciated, bald-headed body was shaking and her T-shirt was soaked through.

The prophet Ezekiel, speaking on behalf of God, proclaimed: "I will take the stony heart out of their flesh and give them a heart of flesh, that they may walk in my statutes and keep my ordinances, and they will be my people, and I will be their God." My mother was dying, and I couldn't feel a thing other than my own profound sense of dislocation and loneliness.

My wonderful, wise Baton Rouge therapist—the same one who urged me to ask God to let me feel His fatherly love—once told me that, at a certain point, the goal of religion and the goal of therapy become the same: to enable the individual to live life fully, and without remorse. You don't want to go to your deathbed regretting that you had missed out on even one of life's manifold blessings. (This is the same message delivered by Pippin's grandmother in the musical *Pippin*, when she sings, "Oh, it's time to start living! Time to take a little from this world we're given! Time to take time, 'cause spring will turn to fall, in just no time at all.") In Judaism, the Torah is viewed as a gift that enables those who follow it to live a full, joyous life—a life without regret. Which is why the first thing my mother did when she began to feel better was go out for lobster—which might not seem particularly in accordance with Torah (lobster being *treyf*), but made perfect sense for my unbelieving but very Jewish mother. Paradise is here, and in the details: in the smell of autumn, the warmth of a down quilt, the breath of your grandchild on your cheek. Every night, Mom had a Jack Daniels, followed by a big supper. "Bourbon's keeping me alive," she said.

But some months before my bat mitzvah, Mom called to say that the cancer that had never, in fact, gone entirely away had started growing again. "It was only a matter of time," she explained as nonchalantly as if she were talking about the price of gasoline, or a change in the weather. Soon her social life began to revolve around the women she saw every Tuesday at her oncologist's office in Fairfax—the women who, like Mom, were battling ovarian cancer. There they sat, a half-dozen or so of them, of varying ages, races, and religions, and chatted, like women in a beauty shop, while the poisons intended to prolong their lives seeped into their veins. Nothing was off-limits, and so they talked, among themselves, about how sex had become unpleasant if not downright impossible and about how their bowel movements, once so reliable, had now become theaters of pain. They talked about how their kids were coping with their illnesses, and about God, and about what kind of funerals they wanted to have, and every once in a while, one of them died, and a new woman took her place. As for my mother, she became the Mother Superior of the group, by virtue both of having survived cancer longer than any of the rest of them had and her more advanced age. Some of the women, she told me, were deeply religious, practically glowing with faith. But she herself simply couldn't embrace the notion that a deity of any sort, let alone a loving deity, was running things. And as for the biblical God—the God of Abraham, Isaac, and Joseph—she considered Him to be no more than the collective projection of generations of emotionally insecure Jewish men. For her, Judaism was *Jewishness:* big pot-roast suppers, bagels and lox, a kind of warm, cozy, loving family togetherness, à la *Fiddler on the Roof*—never mind that the real shtetl was hardly a barrel of laughs, Yiddish expressions weren't a part of the family lexicon, and my siblings and I had been raised in a place where we were the only Jews for miles around. She'd long since put in an order for an only quasi-Jewish funeral—a few Hebrew prayers are okay, she'd said, but forget about wrapping her body in a shroud or having her family sit on the floor, in mourning, during all the seven days of shivah. "And don't forget," she reminded me every now and then. "No black. I want to be buried wearing my star-spangled sweat suit."

"Don't you think that planning your own funeral is a bit perverse?" I'd say, but Mom, ignoring me, would then go on to tell me not to forget about Binky.

"She's not going to have anyone to lean on. I'm counting on you to stay by her side during my funeral, do you understand?"

"Gotcha."

"And another thing. At my funeral, I don't want some Orthodox rabbi I've never met doing a bunch of Hebrew prayers that no one understands, and I don't care what your father says, he can go to his Orthodox synagogue later and pray until the cows come home. Remember, it's my funeral, and most of my friends aren't religious. And another thing: I want lots of food. You and your sisters are going to have to plan it all, because your father—well, you know your father. And for God's sake don't be cheap about it. Call Ridgewell's, they do a good job, and remember that people are always hungry after a funeral."

"Fine, Mom."

"I really mean it about Binky," Mom would then say, bouncing back and forth between her twin obsessions. "She works too hard. That's the problem. She's always in that office of hers. What's she trying to prove? You know what the problem is? The problem is that she's just like your father, and always has been, right from the very beginning. Work, work, work. And you know what your father's problem is? *His* father. Pop did nothing all day but worry about business, and your father swore he'd be different. But what good does it do, working so hard? How is she going to meet someone nice if all she does is work? And after I'm dead? I know that being single isn't a tragedy, but I just hate to see her so alone. Promise me, Jennifer? Promise me that you'll look after her?"

My mother was so anxious about Binky that I could feel her anxiety over the phone, like little currents of goopy, stagnant electricity coming through the earpiece. Forget cancer. My mother was going to die from worrying. And at the rate she was going, she'd take me down with her. I'd hang up, emotionally exhausted, and soon discover that—during our phone conversation—I too had sprouted a tumor. Then I'd have to lie on the bed, poke and prod myself all over a few times, and finally call Stuart in a total panic to see whether he thought it was likely that the cluster of small lumps I had found in my inner thighs was a sign of cancer, the kind that comes on you all of a sudden—sort of the reverse of the idea of spontaneous remission—or whether, instead, I needed to go to the gym more often.

So it really was a good thing when Binky announced that she'd met someone. Specifically, she said that she'd met someone named Matt, who was nice and smart and cute, and who liked her. For the next two months, my mother called me every day to see if I'd heard anything more about Matt, which I hadn't, because Binky wasn't giving out any more information. Then Binky called to ask me if I could come to New York for a black-tie event. She and Matt were married by a rabbi under the chuppah, on a beautiful, starry, very cold, velvet-black night, with families and friends in attendance. Mom wore a bright red dress. She danced all evening, and in photographs of the event, she looks like a woman in love.

Every Shabbat, in synagogue, we pray:

> Honor thy mother and thy father;
> Rejoice with bride and bridegroom;
> Visit the sick;
> And the study of Torah is equal to them all, because it leads to them all.

For months, I'd kept my bat mitzvah plans a secret from everybody but Rabbi Stan, Stuart, and my kids, partly because I felt so geekily self-conscious about it, partly because I was afraid to let anyone know, and partly because, with all the excitement over Binky's wedding, I felt weird telling people that I had an event coming up too. When I finally worked up the courage to tell my father, I did it via e-mail.

"Mommy and I will be sure to be there," my father e-mailed back. Then he began to send me books—so many that I lost count: there were books on Jewish history, ritual, and theology, with titles like *Be'er HaGola: The Classic Defense of Rabbinic Judaism through the Profundity of the Aggadah, The Essential Talmud, A Guide to Rashi's Commentary, Creation According to the Midrash Rabbah, Back to the Sources, The Encyclopedia of Jewish Prayer.* I felt like I was the charter member of the You've-Got-To-Be-Kidding Club. But I loved getting these books: just holding them in my hands filled me with a sense of well-being. Not that I understood them or had any intention of grappling with much more than their flap copy. ("Compellingly demonstrates how R. Soloveitchik joined intellectual brilliance in Jewish learning with a deep empathy of modern existentialist philosophy," says Professor Yuda Gellman of Ben-Gurion University of the Negev about *Love and Terror in the God Encounter*.)

I recently read the Israeli novelist Amos Oz's remarkable memoir *A Tale of Love and Darkness*. In it he recounts how, as a child, he'd simply devoured books. He read with such ferocity that the neighborhood bookseller lent him up to two or three books a day, on the condition that he return them unsullied. My writer friends report much the same thing, telling of childhoods spent curled up in comfortable chairs with everyone from Jules Verne to E. B. White to Chaucer. My own children have this same book-hunger, particularly my son Jonathan, who sometimes goes through a book a day. But when I was a child, I read little, and then without much appetite. In all, I preferred television, comic books, and lying around the house thinking of how sorry everyone was going to be at my funeral to reading books, which required that you be able to concentrate. Looking back on it, I'm pretty sure that the problem wasn't that I lacked imagination, rather, focus. It wasn't until I was in college that I became a serious reader. Now I take books so personally that I am constantly at risk from them, like a vulnerable child at the hands of a dictatorial teacher. Because what if, for example, the book you take with you on vacation is bad and you're too lazy to drive an hour into the nearest town to find a better one? Or what if a friend gives you a copy of *Tuesdays with Morrie*, explaining that it's one of the most "profound and moving" books she's ever read, when you know full well—from having read the first two chapters of this superficial piece of junk one afternoon when you were stuck at your husband's second cousin's house trying to make nice—that *Tuesdays with Morrie* is a Hallmark card stretched out over a couple of hundred of pages, only without any drawings of cute little animals, and that—and this is the point—God doesn't just come slamming into your life, one two three, here I am, time to boogie, let's rock and roll, like He does to the author of *Tuesdays with Morrie?* I mean, what do you *do* with that? Do you tell your friend that you really don't want to hang out with her anymore? Or do you take your husband's advice and forget about it, your friend's taste in books may be different from yours, but since when is that the end of the world?

I really do love to read, and can't imagine anything worse than life without books (except maybe life without hamburgers), but I tend to go for books with plot: novels, histories, biographies, memoir. So every time I saw a UPS truck pull up to the curb, I felt like I was trapped in that bad dream where it's the day of the final exam, only you kind of forgot to attend even a single lecture. When Dad called to ask me what I thought about, for example, Gershom Sholem's descriptions of kabbalistic emanation theory, I'd mumble something along the lines of "interesting," and then claim that I had to go and scrape a kid off the sidewalk or take Sam to the orthodontist. Maybe he could hear the panic in my voice, because about two months before my big day, Dad started sending me the kinds of books that I live for: the marvelous, multigenerational saga *The Radetzky March* by the Jewish Austrian writer Joseph Roth, *Embers* by Sandor Marai, the beautiful, lyrical *The Talmud and the Internet* by Jonathan Rosen (a book that isn't, incidentally, about either the Talmud or the Internet), I. J. Singer's fabulous soap opera, *The Brothers Ashkenazi*. Inside every book, my father wrote *im ahova, m' Abba* (with love, from Daddy) in his square, squat Hebrew script, until, at a certain point, I began to believe him.

In the meantime, I was studying for my bat mitzvah in much the same manner that every Jewish girl studies for her bat mitzvah, by practicing, and practicing, and practicing, reciting the Hebrew prayers over and over again until my kids could no longer stand me and my neighbors began to suspect that I had become a member of a cult. And this is really embarrassing, but another reason I wanted to become a bat mitzvah was because I thought it would make great copy, and I was still so desperate to make my mark that in my mind I'd begun to map out an entire book on the subject, starting with the title. *A Journey Toward Adolescence?* No. How about: *Mitzvah in Mid-Life? A Bat Mitzvah Menopause? Mitzvah in the Middle?* By the time I came up with a title—I think it was *Coming of Age in Middle Age: A Journey on the Torah Path*—I'd realized that such a book, even if I managed to inject humor in it, would at best be boring, because the fact of the matter was that studying for my bat mitzvah mainly entailed sheer, rote memorization, punctuated by bouts of terror. What I did was really no different than what every bar and bat mitzvah kid does, only in my case, I had to deal with my children, who liked to make such helpful comments as "You suck, Mom." I drove out I-12 to sit with my

Hebrew teacher, Charles, in his kitchen, where I went over my Torah and *haftorah* portions, feeling inept while he explained the cantillation to me, expounded on the various permutations of the Hebrew verb *shelach* (send), chatted with his dogs in Hebrew and French, and told me dirty jokes. I schlepped my beat-up scribbled-in copy of the prayer book with me to the Huey P. Long Pool, where my twins had swimming lessons, and to the Baton Rouge Speech and Hearing Foundation, where Jonathan had speech therapy, and to soccer practice and baseball games and dance classes. I sat on our living room sofa and studied under the gaze of my grandfather's grandparents. When I was sent there by a newspaper to do a travel story, I took my prayer book to Jamaica, where I sat under an umbrella on the beach, practicing the *Amida* and the *Kaddush*, while Jamaican waiters in white linen came by and asked me if I'd like a refill on my mai tai. And then there was the Torah portion itself, which I would be chanting, out loud, in front of actual people, a prospect that completely terrified me, be-cause, and this was the problem: what if I fucked up?

Clinging to my consciousness during all this was—big surprise—my father, and his father before him, and so on, going all the way back to Sinai. My father's Germanic family in Baltimore was rigid, ritualistic, and huge—life revolving around Judaism on the one hand and the increas-ingly less profitable hat factory on the other. There were regular Sabbath luncheons with the rest of the extended family of grandparents, aunts and uncles, great-aunts and great-uncles, and assorted first cousins and distant cousins, some of whom were recent arrivals from Germany—having fled as Hitler gained power—who spoke English with thick German accents. And in all the praying, and eating, and worrying about Hitler, in all the Hebrew, and davening, and pride in maintaining the Orthodoxy of their ancestors, there was never any discussion about God. It was almost as if, despite His relentless appearance in the Jewish liturgy, His existence was confined to a historic memory or a reflex, a kind of tribal, Tourettic tic.

Actually, my grandfather was a deeply faithful man. But it wasn't until I was in my forties that I learned that my grandfather believed in God. "A world without God doesn't make sense," he had told my young father one day as the two of them walked to shul. But he never spoke of God again.

By the time I was born, in 1959, the hat factory was gone, and my father's father was rigid, impatient, and most of all, *old*, an easily annoyed, angry presence seated at the end of the dining room table, racing through the Hebrew prayers as if in a marathon, but unwilling to skip even a single verse in the interest of liberating his squirming grandchildren. How rote it all seemed! How denuded, despiritualized, flattening, as if the whole point of the exercise was merely getting through it, in the name of—what? My Orthodox grandfather seemed to do things entirely by the book; he was like a soldier in the service of Emperor Franz Josef, serving a cause that had already died. But my father's family stuck with the old ways even as great swaths of upwardly mobile German Jewish Baltimoreans abandoned them in favor of the more "enlightened" and "American" Reform movement, and they themselves got so rich that they busted first out of downtown and then uptown Baltimore and, along with everyone else who could afford it, moved to what they called "the country," which to my eyes looked a lot like the suburbs, with single-family homes set back from the road on manicured expanses of green grass.

Naturally, it was my father who presided over our own Shabbat dinners in McLean and who also insisted that no daughter of his was going to go out on Friday night—Friday night was the Sabbath, family time, you were a Jew, end of story. On Saturday morning, he jumped in his dark-green Thunderbird and took off for shul, which, unfortunately for the rest of us, was not only miles away, in Georgetown, but also Orthodox, which meant, for starters, that the men and boys sat downstairs while the women and girls sat upstairs, behind a railing. And behind that railing I occasionally sat, with my mother and my sisters, all of us wearing specially bought Yom Kippur hats, looking down on the praying men as, swaying and chanting, they communicated with *Ha Shem*. My mother, who didn't know a lick of Hebrew and didn't have much use for synagogue services of any stripe, was bored silly, but for a few years she put on a good face, comforting herself, I suppose, with thoughts of how nice we all looked in our new High Holiday dresses. But Dad loved synagogue, in part, no doubt, because it reminded him of his boyhood in Baltimore, and in part because, unlike the rest of us, he knew what the Hebrew prayers meant. (He eventually became fluent in Modern Hebrew as well.) Actually, Dad didn't belong to just the Georgetown shul. He also belonged to three others: Chizuk Amuno, in Baltimore, where generations of my father's family had worshipped; Rodef Shalom, a Reform temple in nearby Falls Church, Virginia, which Dad signed us up for when it became clear that, if we were to have any religious instruction at all, it was Temple Rodef Shalom or nothing (for me, it turned out to be nothing, as I regularly played hooky from Sunday school, preferring to be on the lam than stuck inside a classroom learning about the happy lives of the happy, wholesome kibbutzniks in the Land of Israel); and Tefereth Israel on 16th Street in Washington, a conservative shul whose rabbi had been trained in Baltimore by my father's childhood cantor, the beloved Abba Weisgal. It was as if it rested on my father's shoulders, alone, to keep the entire Jewish tradition going. All this left me more than a little puzzled, for despite the torturous experiment in Sunday school attendance at Temple Rodef Shalom, I didn't know an *aleph* from a *bet*, nor did I know, precisely, what Torah was—a fairly central question, at least for Jews, as Torah, in a nutshell, is the Jewish path to God, an eternal teaching that *is* God's love for His People.

In Judaism, you never complete your education, never stop grappling with God and God's will for humankind, which is a fairly daunting idea if, like me, you're a bit of a clean-freak, the kind who likes to finish things, check them off your to-do list, and pack them away. However, in an example of Jewish getting-to-the-point that every Sunday school kid learns, the first-century sage Rabbi Akiva taught: "The great principle of Torah is expressed in the commandment: Love your neighbor as you love yourself; I am the Lord (Leviticus 19:18)." Unfortunately, after he made this pronouncement, Rabbi Akiva added: "Now go and study." Would I ever be finished? Would I ever know enough? Would I ever make the grade? How old did I have to be before I might please my Orthodox ancestors? At what point—if any—would I be able to say, "Enough"?

After college, when I was living in New York, I often found myself wandering around the Lower East Side, mainly out of pure curiosity: I wanted to see if I could imagine myself into the life that had teemed there a hundred years earlier, when tens of thousands of primarily Yiddish-speaking Eastern European and Russian Jewish immigrants had lived in poverty in the tenements south of Canal Street. Mainly I didn't get much past the vendors hawking potato knishes and, if it were winter, how cold I was—and in any event, my own ancestors had come over long before the Lower East Side became Jewish, and they'd settled either in Baltimore or in small towns in the middle South. Every now and again, I'd pass a Hasidic Jew in sidecurls and a black suit, and, my imagination sparked, I'd start down the road of *teshuva:* return. How wonderful, I thought, to exist in a world of such certainty that practically every moment is accounted for, a world devoid of striving, and personal ambition, and chaotic emotions: a world devoted to God. Sometimes the passing Hasid would glance my way, as if he could tell what I was thinking, but more often than not he didn't notice me, which was probably a good thing, as I didn't want to be pegged as half-baked, or, worse, dragged into a Lubavitcher mitzvah mobile to learn about the teachings of the rebbe or how to light *Shabbos* candles. And what if, one day, I actually went ahead and allowed myself to be cajoled into one of those portable, moving mini-yeshivas, staffed by nutcases clothed in the garb of eighteenth-century Polish nobility? Would I be filled with Light? If so, would I have to burn all my miniskirts? Throw out my prized Via Spigas? Give up my daily installment of *Family Ties* on TV?

I never did allow myself to be lured into a mitzvah mobile, but I continued to wander around the city, just drifting from neighborhood to neighborhood, infatuated by all the possibilities multiplying around me, in love with the streets themselves: the sidewalks, the buildings, the smell of the gray sky and the smell of automobile exhaust. Sometimes I took a friend with me, but usually I went in the company of my small stuffed elephant, Elephant. (He rode on top of my keys and wallet in my handbag, looking out.) On one occasion, however, I went with my father. It must have been a Sunday, because I remember that he was wearing painter's pants and an old sweatshirt, with white sneakers, but what he was doing in the city on a Sunday afternoon escapes me. The two of us wandered awkwardly—my father not talking much except to make the occasional remark about American Jewish history, me chattering on about nothing whatsoever, trying to fill up the silence, trying to find a way to him, and simultaneously sinking under the certainty that the more I talked, the more my father yearned to get away from me. Eventually we came to a bookstore. Inside, the shelves were crowded with works in Hebrew, Yiddish, Russian, and English, and these my father perused while I stood near the door, thinking about what I'd wear to work the next day, and if I'd ever get a promotion, which was looking increasingly doubtful. I could hear my father humming as he browsed. The bookstore's owner, in beard and tzitzit, ignored us. Finally Dad approached me, a book in his hand. "Let's get you a Torah," he said. He bought it, murmured a blessing, and handed it to me. The cover showed green leafy vines growing against a marbled purple backdrop. I'd never read it before.

Later that afternoon, back in my apartment on 19th Street, I opened the book and began to read the introduction: in it, the translator noted that the Talmud itself warns against translation, stating: "One who translates a verse literally is misrepresenting the text. But one who adds anything of his own is a blasphemer." When I read these words, I thought: *again* with the you-can't-do-this-*and*-you-can't-do-that? But I delved in anyway, struggling through the boring passages, persevering through the lists of names, ignoring all the punishments by stoning and by drowning, and getting all choked up when I got to the part where Abraham answers God's calling, saying, "Here I am." By the time, weeks later, that I got to the end, when Moses is denied entry to the Promised Land and dies, I was so upset that I ended up throwing myself on the bed, outraged by the utter unfairness of it all, and it wasn't until my roommate, Lissa, knocked on the door to ask me if I wanted to go out for Chinese that I managed to pull myself together again. Later, when Stuart and I traveled to Israel and I saw with my own eyes the places where many of the stories in the Bible took place, and also discovered that much of what is recounted in the Bible is based, to an astonishing degree, in historical and archeological reality, it was as if a whole new world had opened up before me, sort of like it does for Lucy in *The Lion, the Witch, and the Wardrobe* when she walks past the fur coats in the old professor's wardrobe and lands in Narnia. I walked through Hezekiah's tunnel and landed in the book of Kings; touched Solomon's Western Wall; saw the coins minted during the reign of King Jeroboam and the ivories used in Samarian pagan worship services after the Kingdom of David was split into two. Over there, past the Temple Mount, was the Valley of Gehinah, and over there, in the distance, was Mount

Moriah, where Abraham heard and obeyed the call from God. *Hyneni,* he said, hearing the voice of God's angel: *Here I am.*

Every now and then, as I studied for my bat mitzvah in Baton Rouge, I would look up to the heavens, and, like Abraham, say *hyneni.* Then I'd wait for God to let me know what He had in mind for me. Sometimes, I'd feel a little shiver of excitement, a flush of emotion, but as for the booming voice, speaking in clear, well-enunciated American English—sort of like Russell Baker in his *Masterpiece Theatre* introductions—it never came. I kept studying anyhow. What choice did I have? My bat mitzvah was on the synagogue calendar.

A week or so before the Sabbath that I was scheduled to become a bat mitzvah, Dad telephoned to say that he was bringing his father's tallit (prayer shawl) for me. This was the same tallit that my grandfather—my rigid, judgmental, Orthodox, intimidating, imposing, Old World grandfather—had worn when he himself had become a bar mitzvah in 1899, at Chizuk Amuno in Baltimore. My father had worn it on the occasion of his bar mitzvah in 1941, again at Chizuk Amuno, and for the second time in 1991, for the fiftieth anniversary of that event. My brother wore it when he became a bar mitzvah in 1973. My male cousins had also worn it. But no woman in my family had ever become a bat mitzvah: I was the first.

It's hard for me to write about meaningful things—or, for that matter, anything—without cracking jokes,. partly because somewhere along the line, I either had to get funny or I was going to get dead, if not physically dead, a suicide, then spiritually and emotionally so, buried alive under a mountain of shame and self-loathing. So I got funny, and then I wrote an entire funny book about the totally not funny subject of my mother's cancer, and then I decided that if I was going to make my way in the world at all, if I was ever going to have any kind of real, actual, tangible success, it would be through my ability to crack jokes and make wise. But my bat mitzvah wasn't funny. It was hard. And when it was over, I was vastly relieved and extremely exhausted.

Thinking that a large number of my fellow congregants would be out of town for the holiday, and therefore unable to attend services at Beth Shalom, I'd purposefully chosen the Sabbath after Thanksgiving for my bat mitzvah, a choice I immediately regretted by the time I'd finished with chanting my Torah and *haftorah* portions and was onto my speech, which was the part I'd mainly been looking forward to all along. I regretted the choice because I've always loved having an audience, and because of Thanksgiving my audience at Beth Shalom wasn't large. But I did have family in attendance, specifically my parents, my mother-in-law, and Binky and her new husband, Matt, as well as Stuart and our three children.

What I remember is that on the Friday before Saturday morning services, while Rabbi Stan was putting me through my paces in the sanctuary, showing me how to hold the Torah and where and when to bless it, Binky and Stuart were arranging blue flowers in glass vases and setting up tables with blue tablecloths and white napkins. I remember that during my last practice, as I carried the Torah around the room, I accompanied myself to the tune of the "Mexican Hat Dance," and Rabbi Stan said, "I don't think I've ever seen anyone do that before." I remember also that that evening was my parents' forty-fifth wedding anniversary and that I gave a toast to them, thanking them for coming all this way, and thanking my mother for still being alive, to which she replied, "Don't mention it." I also remember that my mother moved slowly, but without pain, and that she'd gotten quite heavy. Dad treated her with a gentleness that I hadn't thought possible, and before we all sat down for Friday night dinner, Binky read my speech, which I hadn't allowed anyone else to see, and suggested a small change. I went to bed excited but calm.

On the Shabbat morning of my bat mitzvah ceremony my father took me aside, draped his father's tallit over my shoulders, placed his hands on my head, and recited the traditional blessing for the wearing of the tallit. *Bless my soul, Lord, my God; You are very great; You have donned majesty and splendor; cloaked in light as with a garment, stretching out the heavens like a curtain.* It smelled like old wool and dust and closets and powder, and I wondered what my grandfather would think if he knew that I was wearing his tallit, and hoped he wouldn't be too angry at me. I put a yarmulke on my head, affixing it with a bobby pin. My hair was still very long, and I'd pulled it back into a braid. I could feel my braid tumbling down my back over my grandfather's tallit, heavy like a rope, and my breath pushing against my lungs.

Then the service began.

For any bar or bat mitzvah, there are a lot of expectations, and like any other bar or bat mitzvah, I was nervous and self-conscious. I sat beside Rabbi Stan, sweating bullets, acutely aware of my father, sitting just one row behind me, his painfully off-tune voice throwing me off my own reading, careening into corners that it had no business in, lurching like a drunk, destroying whole worlds of meaning as it crashed and thudded from one *baruch ata* to the next. Aside from his voice, I could feel his physical presence as strongly as I'd felt it when I was a little girl: it was like a force field, simultaneously pushing and pulling me. And there, right beside him as she had been for forty-five years, was my mother, who was then three years from her death and at the very end of her strength. She thought I was crazy. I knew this because she'd told me so. She didn't understand why I'd bother with all that stuff that had driven all of us bonkers back in McLean, and which, even now, in Baton Rouge, often seemed foreign, petrified, and rote. But I also knew—because, again, she'd told me—that she was pleased and also somewhat envious. Envious because I had a shot at doing what she could never quite do, which was to find a home for myself within Judaism. The kids were looking at me with funny little semi-embarrassed expressions on their faces, and Stuart was giving me little nods of his head, as if I were once again in labor and he was standing by my head saying, *It's okay, you'll be fine, you're almost there, you can do it, just one more push, Jen, just one more, there you go!!*

Although there are differences among synagogues, depending on how traditional they are, Shabbat morning services are basically always the same: there are the preliminary, warm-up prayers, then the prayers of thanksgiving, assorted Psalms, and finally the biggies—the Eighteen Benedictions, the Ashrai, the Shema and V'ahafta—and finally the heart of the service, which is the reading from the Torah. Most kids, myself included, manage to master the prayers without too much angst, but reading from the Torah can be daunting, because, unlike in the printed prayer book, Torah scrolls are handwritten, by a scribe, and composed without vowels. In addition, Torah isn't simply read, but chanted, each verse with its own specific trope, which is neither tune nor rhythm but a set, musical chant. You can learn to read trope (as I did for my Torah portion) but the cantillation—the symbols themselves—like the vowels, aren't inscribed in the Torah. You just have to remember them. Which is why you practice.

The Torah service begins with the opening of the Ark. The Torah is taken out and carried through the congregation, like a king or a queen, which is exactly what Judaism regards Torah as being. Congregants shake the rabbi's hand and kiss the Torah as the little procession passes through. As I carried the Torah in my arms, and people turned toward me to shake my hand or offer up a little hug, my parents sat, side by side, quietly wiping away their tears.

My Torah portion was *Chayei Sarah* (the death of Sarah), but I confined myself to only those twenty verses that tell the story of Abraham sending his trusted servant to the land of his fathers to find a daughter of the Hebrews to take as a wife for Isaac. The chapter ends just as the servant has spied Rebecca at the well. The verses of the Prophets that I chanted told the story of David's painful relationship to his beloved, treacherous son, Adonijah. So there was a lot of juicy stuff I could expound on, afterward, for my *drash* (teaching), and I had consulted all kinds of sources—from the ArtScroll Tanach commentary on the one hand to www.Talmud.com on the other—but in the end I spoke of more personal things, particularly why, at the age of forty-one, I had finally become a bat mitzvah. I talked about my paternal grandfather, the only one I had ever known, who had loomed so large—the very image of the authentic Jew—in my childhood. I said that there was no doubt in my mind that, had my grandfather still been alive, he would have been shocked, perhaps even disapproving, at the sight of me in his tallit. I said that I could picture him, sitting in the back of the shul, grumbling—women, after all, didn't have much of a role in Judaism beyond producing good meals and sitting on charitable boards. I said that, when I was a child, I was certain that my grandfather didn't like me, in part because I was a girl and in part because he could sense that as a Jew, I was a flop. I left out the parts about how he'd intimidated my mother to the point of frenzy and distrusted Nana for being insufficiently Jewish, but I did say that though my father had always revered his father, I had never felt close to him at all, such that even at his funeral, in 1979, I didn't feel that I had a rightful place among the mourners at his graveside.

But I was wrong about my grandfather. That night, after all the catered food had been wrapped in plastic wrap and shoved to the back of the refrigerator and everyone, including me, was asleep, my grandfather came to me. He stood in the near distance, a quiet, solid figure in a dark suit. There were no words spoken and no gestures made, but I knew that he had come to give me his blessing—a tacit thumbs-up from the next world. And when I woke, I was filled with peace and knew that I had had no ordinary dream, but something closer to a vision or a visitation. Both Stuart and the kids think I'm cracked, but there you have it.

And now, on occasion, I talk to this difficult, anxious, quarrelsome Orthodox Jewish grandfather of mine, this grandfather who believed that a world without God doesn't make sense, and he tells me things that I never knew before, and leaves me with a feeling of being profoundly understood.

11

Where They Landed

Ever since we had moved to Baton Rouge, Stuart had been talking about where he wanted to go once his sabbatical year finally rolled around, and, hating change of any kind, I had been ignoring him. Suddenly, however, his theoretical sabbatical year—the year that he said he wanted to spend in someplace exotic, like India, or perhaps Vietnam—was looming in our immediate-enough future, and we had to make a decision. After talking it to death for months, we finally decided to aim for Scotland, where they at least spoke English (sort of), guns were illegal, and the single malt was heaven. The law faculty of the University of Glasgow offered Stuart a position as a "visiting scholar," which meant that he got an office and a computer but didn't have to actually do any work, and we were set to go. (Stuart ended up writing his first book there.)

Meaning that I now had a to-do list that stretched from one end of the house to the other and then had to be subdivided into categories, crossreferenced, and indexed, and a husband who was making plans to give lectures in places like Oslo and Heidelberg but was essentially useless, utterly incapable of so much as thinking about things like where we might actually live in Scotland or school for the kids. And what if, during our year abroad, Nana up and died? Or if, God forbid, my mother took a drastic turn for the worse? Cancer had long since become the central story of her existence, her raison d'être, a kind of black hole into which everything else fell. She talked about her impending death so much that there were times when I wanted to kill her, just to get it over with. God forbid she chose my year in Scotland to start down her long-promised decline. For me, getting on an airplane represents a triumph of pharmacology over sheer, overwhelming terror. If

Mom started going downhill fast, what was I supposed to do, commute from Glasgow to Washington? How hard would it be for me to get my prescription for Ativan renewed under the British national health plan?

But in the meantime—when my to-do list wasn't sending me into orbit—I felt this vast inner calm, this abiding, wondrous sense that something marvelous had happened to me. Not that I could go around telling the whole world that, by the way, my dead grandfather came and paid me a visit. But I knew that he had, and moreover, as time went on, I knew *why* he had. It was pretty basic, actually: he'd come to thank me for taking Judaism on, for agreeing to live within it and for passing it on to my children.

But I was still cut off from my mother's family, those crazy Southern cousins whom Mom herself didn't know really well, those whose parents, unlike Nana, stayed in the middle South, uninterested in the glories of New York or Washington, Philadelphia or Chicago.

So I was glad when Mardi Gras rolled around and, because the kids had a whole week off of school, we four could ditch Stuart for a few days, leaving him to his plans for Europe and his scholarship. The kids wanted to do something fun, like go to McLean to see their grandparents, but I had a better idea. I wanted to go to Henderson, Kentucky—where Nana had been born and raised, recording her journey in her Memory Books. If I couldn't remember Nana's memories for her, if her story was to be overwhelmed by the stronger tug of my father's family mythology, the least I could do was see the place that shaped and colored her memories—the world of her childhood, in which she now dwelled.

I wrote tons of e-mails and made a bunch of phone calls, and on a beautiful cold Sunday during Mardi Gras, while the rest of the country was in New Orleans, getting drunk, the kids and I met my mother's first cousin, Leon Levy, in front of 400 South Main Street in Henderson: site of Nana's childhood, her engagement party, and her grandmother Augusta's death.

"Y'all made it," Leon said in his slightly tawny mid-South accent, adding, "You look just like your grandmother."

"Thank you."

Then he launched into a family history lesson: The house just down the street from the one Nana had grown up in belonged to Uncle Mike, who had a drugstore on the other side of town and who rode to work and back on his bicycle until the age of ninety-two, when he retired. Aunt Hortence, who was Nana's mother's sister from Brownsville, Tennessee, had a reputation for being a birdbrain, but she bought real estate downtown, and made a pile. She married Alex Mayer, whose brother Carl was driving the car in 1919, when it crashed, killing Nana's father, Lee. Aunt Jennie (after whom, apparently, Nana was named) and Lee's brother, Uncle Henry, lived right next door, at number 402: he worked with his brother in his brother's furniture store. When Nana's daddy died, Uncle Henry took over the business, only he was a drunk and a gambler, and he pissed away the profits on the ponies and eventually lost the store. Cornelia Weil—who was Aunt Hattie's sister-in-law—lived across the street, only she was as mean as a snake. All this Leon told me within the first ten minutes after our arrival, as we stood on the sidewalk in the cold sunshine.

On and on he went, intermingling his own memories with bits of family history and weaving the family history around the larger story of Jews in the South, their growing sense of being full-fledged Americans, and his own sense of loss. His father (Nana's brother, Henry, my late great-uncle) had had a failing farm in Brownsville, and apparently his favorite trick was terrorizing his family whenever the mood struck him, which, because he was an alcoholic, was often. But in Henderson, Leon explained, things were done on the up and up. "And let me tell you," Leon said, "when Mommy Les said 'jump,' you jumped." He fingered the small Star of David pendant that he wore on a silver chain around his neck and gazed toward the Ohio River.

The town itself was almost exactly as Nana had described it to me. The river, along whose banks Nana had once collected Indian arrowheads, which she then traded with her friends the way my sons trade baseball cards, is visible from the front stoops of just about any house along the wide boulevard of Main Street. The downtown area is still thriving, even prosperous, its handsome brick nineteenth-century buildings exuding an aura of certainty. The large building on the corner of North Elm and First Street, once my great-grandfather's furniture and hardware store, is still in use as a furniture store—Alles Brothers—and the bank building on Main Street, on the third floor of which Nana's stepfather, Sol Heilbronner, practiced law, is still operating as a bank. Proud houses rise up the hill beyond Main Street, but beyond the hill—literally on the other side of the tracks—is a neighborhood of mainly small, mainly shabby houses, dwellings that have the forlorn look of stray dogs and seem perched only precariously on their foundations, as if waiting for the next big wind to blow them off the face of the earth: this is the black side of town, where the women who worked in Nana's mother's house lived and their children and grandchildren now live. But as far as the Jews went—there were no Jews. All the Jews were either scattered to distant cities or resting beyond the city limits, in the Jewish cemetery.

There, in the Jewish cemetery, I finally made contact with my mother's ancestors, that vast family of playful, imaginative, and creative storytellers who had spread out all over the mid-South in the years following the Civil War. While the kids played tag among the shadows, I walked from grave to grave, over the bones of the people whose photographs adorn my stairwell in Baton Rouge. Here was my great-grandmother, lying between my great-grandfather ("Daddy Lee") and her second husband, Sol. There lies Nana's first cousin Dorothy Freeman, the one who had killed herself with her father's gun upon her return to college in Virginia after Christmas vacation. She died in 1928. Beside her is her mother, Hattie. Here, too, are my grandmother's father's parents, Moses and Augusta Levy—Augusta, whom my grandmother called "Henderson Grandma," was born on Christmas day in 1838 and died on Christmas day ninety years later. The day before she died, she'd been keenly discussing the Kellogg treaty. I know this because I have a clipping of her obituary from the Henderson newspaper.

I wanted to recite the mourner's kaddish, and told Sam to run back to the minivan to grab his prayer book—which he had with him on the theory that he was supposed to be studying for his own upcoming bar mitzvah—but Sam said that he didn't need it. He knew the prayer by heart. Wearing the New York Yankees baseball cap that never left his head, he recited the kaddish over the graves of his long-dead ancestors. *Yitgadal v' yitkadash, sh'mei rabbaw.* May His great Name be exalted and sanctified in the world that He created as He willed. May He give reign to His kingship in your lifetimes and in your days and in the lifetimes of the entire family of Israel, swiftly and soon. And let us say: Amen.

His words floated over the graves and lifted into the trees, as I stood there beside my mother's cousin, feeling all goofy and good inside, as if Big Bird had stepped out of the television set to enfold me in his bright yellow, feathery wings. But Sam wasn't interested in lingering over his own role in what, in my mind, had become a formulation about the chain of generations, or, for that matter, in his mother's mother's mother's ancestors. He finished the prayer, smiled, and then ran across the graves to tackle his little brother, who was standing at the edge of the woods, spacing out. The two of them rolled around in the leaves, wrestling like Jacob and the angel.

A few months later, our plane swooped toward the Highlands and touched down in a mist. We took a taxi to our new house, met our new neighbors, learned to drive on the wrong side of the road, bought school uniforms, ate fish and chips, traveled. Bit by bit, the discomfiture I felt from having uprooted myself faded and was replaced first by a feeling of general well-being, and then by this kind of heart-quickening entrancement. I woke each morning eager to get to my computer. I met Debra, an American living full-time in Glasgow, who quickly became one of those once-in-a-decade friends. She and I met for lunch or coffee, and I'd laugh so hard that my stomach hurt. In the afternoons I walked through the Botanic Gardens, under brilliant blue skies and gold and red foliage, to pick up the children from school; afterward we would go to the local shops— the fishmonger's, the cheese shop, the fruit stall—to buy ingredients for that night's dinner. And everything was so safe, and everyone was so friendly, and the city itself, with its red sandstone Victorian mansions and wide green parks, was beautiful. I was in love.

Then I found a lump in my left breast. Stuart assured me that, like all the other lumps in all my various body parts that I'd found over the years, this one, too, would turn out to be nothing. But this time it wasn't nothing.

It was cancer.

12

God's Arms Are Very Long

There is a bed available for me in the Western Infirmary, Glasgow, a place filled with people who say "wee," as in "Will you have a wee tea, then?" and "You mean this wee tiny lump here?" It's so drab that I am already deciding how I will describe it to my friends in the States: as a hospital out of the Gulag perhaps? Or something left over from the Great War? Already I'm planning on telling them: "Even if I survive the cancer, I might have to commit suicide just to get out of this place." The acoustic ceiling tiles are stained and falling in. The linoleum is peeling. The walls are covered with ancient pea-green paint, cracked and streaked with water stains. The molded plastic chairs date from the early sixties and come in colors that shouldn't exist: avocado, aqua, pumpkin-orange. The one pay phone is in the dayroom, itself decorated with unmatching chairs in various stages of decomposition. The windows are filthy, which is a shame, because the views of Glasgow from the tenth-floor ward (breast cancer and general surgery) are magnificent: to the south, the River Clyde and the sprawl of what was once the might of industrial, dirty Glasgow; to the north the sandstone tenements of the West End climbing up the hills and glowing in the sun as if on fire.

As if having cancer isn't enough, I have roommates: three, to be exact. Fiona, in the next bed, is a trim blond with a worried face and a breathless, whispery way of speaking. She's always hot. At night, when I'm huddling under the blankets, hugging myself for warmth, Fiona is resting under a single bedsheet, while an oscillating fan, placed above her bed, makes whirring sounds like rain falling. Perhaps she is going through menopause, but I am unable to confirm this one way or another. Fiona is fifty-three: a fairly standard age for menopause. I, however, am only forty-three, the baby of the group. Fiona's husband died more than twenty years ago, of cancer, in this very same hospital. Fiona recognizes some of the oncology nurses from then. "So I guess you figure that you've had enough shit dropped on you for one lifetime?" I ask her on the third day of our being neighbors in the two beds on the west side of the room. "Something like that," Fiona says.

Jean is in the bed opposite my own. She's in her early sixties, a retired nurse. Five years ago it was the left breast that came off. This time it's the right one. But as she repeatedly says: "At least I'm even." She also tells anyone within hearing distance that now that she has no chest at all she can see how big her tummy is. She has three grown sons—the children of her husband—and many grandchildren, who make her get-well cards. She tells us of their exploits. They are good children. Just before she is wheeled off for surgery, she looks up from her pillow and says: "Don't forget to put my dentures back in before you take me upstairs." She has a pile of trashy magazines by her bed: British tabloids, gossip magazines with photographs of Princess Diana's butler's house, Cherie Blair, and various movie stars and singers. She also reads the junky, slightly right-wing *Daily Mail,* whereas I read the *New York Times* and the *Baton Rouge Advocate* on the web, and now also read either the *Herald* or the *Guardian,* depending on what Stuart picks up on his way home from the university where he is ensconced this year—this much looked-forward-to sabbatical year—in an office overlooking the ancient university chapel, with its stained-glass windows and soaring spire. The *Guardian* is a better paper, but it sometimes lapses into such politically correct posturing that in recent weeks I have done nothing but write letters to the editor, protesting its stand on everything from the Middle East to the Midwest. None of my letters to the *Guardian* have been published.

Liz is the same age as Jean, but because her short, boyish hair is white-white, without a trace of underlying blond or gray, her eyebrows are similarly white, and bushy, and her long, slender body is somewhat shapeless; because she hums while she does needlework and talks about getting a nice cup of tea, I think of Liz as being the grandmother of the group. She snores, loudly, but this doesn't bother me much, as I'm zonked out on painkillers. I sum her up and decide that of my three roommates, Liz is the one I am least likely to feel any real affection for or have any real bond with. Liz has had one breast removed, prompting Jean to say that she will now feel like she has a "spare tire," which prompts me to say, "a spare tire and a flat tire." A few hours after her surgery, Liz was visited by one of the hospital chaplains. He closed the curtains around the bed. I felt a small wave of envy. I wanted my own crew, my own spiritual advisor—my rabbi, my therapist, my friends. The next day, Liz padded in her nightgown over to my bed and recited a verse from Deuteronomy.

> It is the Lord who goes before you.
> He will be with you;
> he will not fail you or forsake you.
> Do not fear or be dismayed.

She said that when she went into surgery she had this verse taped on her stomach and another one, from the gospels, taped on her thigh, explaining that she was born a Catholic but had become a Baptist. She wears a series of silky, sexy nightgowns in soft colors—peach, cream—trimmed with lace, and when her husband comes to see her, every night when he gets off from work, he brings the smell of coldness into the room, and a sense of peculiarly male bewilderment.

Was it really just a few days ago that I returned to the doctor's to be told that the small lump I'd found a week earlier was malignant? Was that me sitting, half-dressed and trembling, while a young, gentle surgeon, his face composed into an expression of professional sympathy, explained that surgery would remove the tumor and a small donut of flesh around it and then said that I was lucky, that the tumor was small, the size of a pea, or a small pearl, that tumors caught this early in the game are usually well contained within the breast? Can this really be me lying here in this bed, an NHS hospital bracelet fastened around my left wrist, praying and praying—dear God if You exist—to be spared an early death?

Because the thing is, despite my lifelong hypochondria: I'm not a candidate for cancer at all, let alone a candidate for a cancer that's virulent enough to require chemotherapy, which I've been told is a distinct possibility, though I won't know for sure until the lab work comes back. Chemotherapy is something I happen to know a thing or two about but seems an impossibility for me, something that I simply, and fundamentally, couldn't survive. How my mother has done it all these years, going back for more, and then more again, I can't say. And anyway, the whole deal is like some bad vaudeville act—so did I tell you the one about the mother and the daughter who had cancer at the same time?

My father, ever the optimist, calls me and says: "I know women who have gone through this. It'll be one, two, three, and you'll be out of there."

My mother, however, does not know what is happening, does not yet know that her second daughter, the who has done everything right—has nursed her three babies and stopped drinking coffee, has taken up yoga, weighs the same as she did in college, and almost always chooses fish over meat—is lying in a bed on the tenth floor of the Western Infirmary in Glasgow, recovering from having a cancerous tumor removed from her left breast, and praying that the pathology report, when it comes in on Friday, won't be too bad. This is because my mother is once again sick, desperately so—weak as a nursling, unsteady as a twig—and though during our phone conversations she's assured me that there's no need to come home and see her, I can hear how frail she sounds, how tired, how fed up. But my mother, in classic Jewish-mother style, worries about me even when she herself is desperately ill, which has always made me nuts—as if I can't get on with things properly without Mom's vigilant care. I'm almost as worried about telling Mom about my breast cancer as I am about the cancer itself. I tell Dad: "If Mom knows, she'll give me a brain tumor." But Dad has the solution: "Don't tell her," he says.

"Ever?"

"Ever."

Cancer: it's defined my mother for so long, providing a sort of lens through which to refract life, that it's as if no other subject can exist, or at least not for her. But now I understand that I'm like my mother after all, that she inhabits me no matter how far I flee from her, that nothing I can do will separate my fate from hers. She and I are heading for the same place, fast, and once we get there, Nana will come too. Only we're going to go in reverse order: first me, then Mom, and then finally, when she's good and ready, when she's had just about all she can take of her misfiring neurons, my ninety-five-year-old grandmother.

"But she's my mother," I say. "She has to know."

"No, she doesn't," Dad says, and his voice, over the long-distance line, sounds wistful.

How do I explain to my old friends, my friends from college and New York, that I need their prayers? Do I just blurt it out? Since moving to Baton Rouge, my vocabulary has undergone a radical change, and that change, in turn, has shaped my thinking. I no longer ask myself: What should I do? But rather: What does God intend for me? How can I best serve Him? I no longer think: Where did I come from? But rather: Where am I going? I've gone from being a brain-heavy East Coast Jewish agnostic to a Southern eccentric who talks out loud to God.

My children are not pleased. How could they be? One minute their mother is worrying about her weight and railing against that cowboy in the White House, and the next minute she's facedown, Muslim-style, talking to God. Not just talking: begging. *Please, dear God, don't let me die.*

They come to visit, bringing the smell of wet wool and rain into the room, piercing its medicinal smells with the sense of urgent, vibrant life. In their school uniforms, they look vaguely like British royalty: gray flannel trousers, school ties, school crests, blazers, and for Rose, a gray flannel skirt with her blazer and scarf. Sam is just thirteen and finally embarking on his bar mitzvah studies for real, studying every Sunday morning with an Orthodox rabbi who doubles as a wine merchant, whom Sam adores. He is just my height and so handsome that I fear for him, with his wide shoulders and narrow waist, his broad, clear forehead, his freckles. His favorite pastime is mimicking his classmates, switching from an Australian to an Indian to a Glaswegian to an English accent before returning to his own, broad American vowels. Rose fusses over me, straightening my bed sheets and telling me not to sit with one leg dangling over the other—didn't the doctors tell us not to cross our legs? She is so purely herself that I often wonder where she came from, though at least a little part of her—her radiant, remarkable beauty—is, I think, a gift from Nana. She looks like neither me nor Stuart, but rather, at nine, has long, straight, thick brown hair, which she pulls back into ponytails, a strong, tall, sturdy body, and a perfect pink mouth. An old soul is what she is, a person who somehow knows exactly how to be within her own skin. Of the three of them, only Jonathan looks even a little bit like me, with his thick, dark brown hair, his wide mouth, and his piercing, dark brown eyes. But the rest of him—from his long, thin body to his sharp knees and elbows to his elegant, Semitic nose—is pure Stuart. Unlike his father, though, Jonathan is always in motion, and talks so rapidly that you're afraid he'll collapse from the sheer force of the wind rushing through his vocal chords. He and Rose are nine. In school, they're memorizing their multiplication tables, something I myself still haven't mastered, having given up on the hard numbers, which for me were eight and twelve, when I was in the fourth grade.

Please, dear God, even if the world doesn't need me for me, even if I never paint another painting or write another word, please let me live for them.

At least until they are eighteen, nineteen . . .

At least until they know who they are . . .

Stuart sits beside me, his long face immobile, as if he were gazing at my coffin or deciding who should deliver my eulogy. His father died of colon cancer many years ago, and he still talks with sadness about the horrors his father endured during radiation. "He'd just lie in bed, moaning and screaming. Mom couldn't take it," he says, looking at me with big mournful eyes in his long, intelligent, sad face, until I have to tell him to stop looking at me as if I'm already dead, or if not dead, nearly so, because if he keeps looking at me like that, surely I'll develop a brain tumor. He's brought work with him: notebooks, pens, thick tomes with titles like *Action and Value in Criminal Law*, and *Lawyers and Justice: An Ethical Study*. As for me, I've brought two novels, my Hebrew text book, Rose's Walkman, Elephant and Bumby, and a whole bunch of Alison Krauss CDs.

My surgeon, who has kind crinkly eyes and a gray beard, noticing that I am sharing my bed, asks what the names of my companions are. "Who are these wee friends?" is how he puts it. "This one," I say, pointing to Elephant's extraordinarily compassionate face, "is Elephant." "Ah," he says. "And this," I add, indicating the small blue lump of raggedy ears and tattered blue fur, "is Bumby." Bumby, I explain, has been with me since I was a toddler, and she is a rabbit. A bunny, actually. Bumby, of course, has her own rather complicated history, but I don't go into that right now. I will save Bumby's story—which is really the story of my own complicated psychic history, all mixed up with my search for God, and for comfort, and for feeling at home in the world—for Debra, who also has a family of stuffed animals. I love Debra. Amazing that I met her just four months ago, at a cocktail party in a beautiful, high-ceilinged, Victorian flat in the West End, the kind of place that's furnished with priceless art, antique Oriental rugs, and books. At that point, we had only been in Glasgow for four days, and going to the cocktail party in the beautiful flat gave me a real-estate envy attack unlike any I had previously known.

I make an executive decision. It's this: if I die, Stuart will have to marry Debra. Debra is smart, funny, compassionate, and my kids are crazy about her. The only problem is she isn't Jewish. Also, she's married.

When she comes to visit, she brings a small, soiled pouch and hands it to me, saying: "I know this isn't much of a gift, but I thought you might be able to use it." Inside are three tiny, discolored, plastic birds with furrowed, cranky expressions on their beaky faces: one is red, one is the blue-turquoise of bathroom tiles, and the third is the color of dirty teeth. "They're Worry Birds," Debra says, explaining that when she was a little girl, she got them out of a vending machine. "They got me this far," she says. "Now you should have them."

One night after dinner, workmen appear in the corridor outside our door. They are ripping up the old linoleum, putting in new. One of them, in a hat and dirty blue jeans, sings beautifully, singing:

> Wide open space
> Take off your shoes, stay out of the race
> Lay down your head on a soft river bed
> Sonny remember the words mamma said

I have been anxious my entire life—so anxious that at times it's all I can do to put one foot in front of the other, or tolerate my three children's childish moods, their enthusiasm, their schoolyard stories, their desire to share their lives with me, their mother. But now the anxiety abates, abates. I sleep with Debra's Worry Birds under my pillow. I do not think about Friday.

The chaplain who finally comes to visit me is Church of Scotland. Previously, when I had put in my request, I'd been asked which denomination I wanted sent to my bedside. "What are my choices?" I replied. "Church of Scotland, Church of England, or Catholic," was the answer. "It doesn't matter," I answered. I have always been nondiscriminating when it comes to clergy, perhaps even a bit promiscuous, figuring, as I always have, that if God exists, as He better, then anyone with a good heart and a specialty in God Relations can help me out. After all, at St. Anthony's, I am showered— and I mean showered—with blessings in the name of Jesus, something that I not only find nonthreatening but actually love. All of which I try to explain to the chaplain, who has an open, friendly face and a sweaty forehead, which he dabs continuously with a handkerchief, only it comes out all wrong. Perhaps because I'm talking so fast, trying to tell everything in two minutes. Or because I'm crying. But the main problem is that what I really want to say to the chaplain is: "Do you think I'm going to die?" Instead, what I say comes out in little unconnected bursts, fragments representing years of experience, run-on sentences. For example, I tell the chaplain the story about how my Catholic psychotherapist in Baton Rouge had suggested that I pray to God to feel His heavenly love and how the very next day the mailman brought me a book, sent from my father, who had inscribed it to me, in Hebrew, "With love from Abba." Coincidence? Or sign from God? The chaplain seems to be impressed. I also tell him about a dream I'd had the previous night, only "dream" is too solid a word to describe what I experienced, which was more like a dozing dream, a semi-waking fantasy, in which I was aware of myself in the role of stage manager and director. In the stage-managed "dream," Ronnie, a friend of ours from Baton Rouge who himself had died of cancer a few years earlier, appeared wearing his characteristic white hat, pants, and shoes, on the balcony of a hotel-motel. In life, Ronnie was a businessman who never quite made it and friend to all who came his way, the son of a large family of Syrian Jews who had come to Baton Rouge from Aleppo in the 1920s and opened a linen shop, Broadway Linens, on Third Street downtown. In death, he was acting as my broker, signaling that he'd try to work something out with God. Finally God himself appeared, looking frail and beat-up, a bit like a bum or a used car salesman, as my Orthodox grandfather (may he rest in peace) might say. For some time it looked like God wouldn't cooperate, but finally He seemed to signal that He'd spare my life if I would promise to return to St. Anthony's.

"So what do you think?" I finally ask the chaplain. "What do you think of my dream?"

"You're obviously a person who dreams a lot and for whom symbolism and narration is important," the chaplain says, disappointingly, and at that very minute, Sam's bar mitzvah teacher—who is also the rabbi of the old, downtown synagogue where we now attend services—walks in. I am a wee bit embarrassed to be seen talking to the other side, but both men, the minister and the rabbi, are terribly polite.

One night, a group of Christmas carolers come through the ward, singing "The First Noel," "Silent Night," and other old faithfuls in chirpy, chipper voices, forced smiles plastered on their faces. Who invited them? I don't know whether to laugh or cry. I tell my roommates: "My theory is that they're all drug addicts, and this is part of their rehab." I also say: "If they sing 'Rudolf the Red-Nosed Reindeer,' I'm going to scream." But Liz says: "I think it's lovely."

Joanna is the night nursing aid. She's big—*big*—with a fat woman's jolly laugh and good humor. Clear white skin. Thick brown hair. "Well, girls, what will it be tonight? A wee dram? Vodka or scotch?" she says. And: "I need to get you girls some sexier knickers." She checks our lines, drains our drains, and fusses about, handing out painkillers, clucking over the exploits of Prince Charles and his horse-faced girlfriend. Joanna: a good name for a nurse, and I think of the other Joanna, the American Joanna, tending the dying in Baton Rouge. I get out my notebook, write myself a note: *Write to St. Anthony's. Ask them to pray for me.*

"Would you look at them, then?" she says, cocking her head in the direction of the earnest, dour carolers. "It's Medieval torture, is what it is."

From her bed on the other side of the room, Jean looks up and says: "Would you get a look at how Princess Di's butler lives? A bit of a toff he is, I should say."

Then she says that once, when she'd first lost her breast, she was taking off her bra but had forgotten how heavy the prosthesis was. "I hit myself in the eye," she says, "nearly knocked myself out."

I have been having visions. Visions like I've never had before. They come at me, day and night, singing. Look up, Jennifer! Open your eyes and *see*!

And I do: I see black women in white hospital gowns floating through the blue air; big, red flowers—tulips, perhaps; golden trees; and God's arms enfolding them all. God has very long arms. They reach all the way from there to here. When I go home, I will paint some of these visions. Just a few weeks before we'd moved to Glasgow, I was up half the night rocketed by one vision after the other and finally had to take a sleeping pill. Later, I wrote a long letter to my friend Richard Brickner, a novelist, telling him that at times I felt that I loved my own creativity more than I loved my own children and that surely this was a sin. Richard called the day he got my letter and said: "You know, of course, that you're setting up a false conflict?" I confessed that I knew. Now Richard calls again, from New York, worried about me. Richard survived a car accident when he was twenty, which left him in a wheelchair, with only partial recovery of his upper limbs. "Frankly," I tell him, "I'd rather have what I have than what you have. That is, if the cancer doesn't kill me." "Well, yes, I agree," Richard answers.

There are other visions, too, intimations, messages. One night I am lying sleepless, when, from inside my own head, I hear a man's voice saying, "I got you, baby, you gon' be all right." Instantly, I know who it is. It's Gerald! Gerald—who died at St. Anthony's years earlier, who told me that he saw an angel coming through the window in his room, and that he, Gerald, *was* the angel. I didn't even manage to get to his funeral. What's he doing in my brain? "Gerald?" I whisper. "Sure 'nuff," he says. "What are you doing here?" There is a pause, and then he says, "I done tol' you that I am an angel. Someone got to look after you. Turns out, it's me. That okay with you? Or you want God to send someone who a sharper dresser?" And on and on he goes like that, cracking jokes, as if my having cancer in a hospital approximately six thousand miles from my own home is the funniest thing he'd ever heard of.

Not that I tell anyone about Gerald. It's bad enough I have cancer. I need my entire family to think I'm having auditory hallucinations too? And perhaps, after all, I am.

One day I sit down and make a list for living: Pray, See my friends, Love my family, Work with faith, Go back to St. Anthony's, Get a dog, Gerald.

"Why," I ask all three of my roommates on our next-to-last night to-gether, "would God give me these gifts if He doesn't want me to use them?" I begin to cry; Liz pads over to give me Kleenex; and the others, all of them, no doubt, thinking of their own torn flesh, their own vivid hopes, murmur words of encouragement. I would like to sit there crying all night long—I love being the center of attention—but just then one of the night nurses comes in with the tea trolley. "Any of you girls wanting a lovely cup of tea?"

The doctor said that the lump was small, but then again, the lump never should have been there anyway. What if it, though small, is filled with an unusually aggressive and deadly form of cancer? What if, despite the movie playing in my head, featuring me, myself, and I as funny, feisty heroine, the cancer spreads and spreads until all that's left of me is a pair of eyes that open and close, until at last they no longer open? In the melo-drama version of my life, wouldn't it be fitting if, just as I am coming into myself—just as I'm working with ease, as if God himself supplied both prose and imagery, and just as the children have reached that sweet age where they still worship us but are old enough to be quite independent— I get zapped? Particularly as, as I will later explain to Stuart, I feel blessed with extraordinarily clear vision, an almost instinctive ability to see into the souls of others? *As if she's prepared to go.* In my own warped version of events, it is just as I'm rising to such heights that I will be stricken, pun-ished, humiliated, ground to dust.

Fiona says: "Don't even go there. Don't let yourself go there."

Jean says: "We go to the peaks and the valleys, you see."

Liz says: "Do you know the story of the two sets of footprints on the beach? And then one set disappears? God is carrying you, and He will not let you down."

But that night, Liz can't sleep. She sits in a chair by the window, listen-ing to the wireless, as she calls it, and humming hymns to herself. At dawn, thinking of her daughter, who is to come up from England to visit her today, she begins to weep.

In my own bed, I hug my knees.

When Stuart visits me, I tell him that I am on the wrong side of the bed. I'm not supposed to be here, I say. I'm supposed to be *there,* in the chair, holding someone else's hand. I'm the one who consoles, who sits by the dying, who makes vague murmuring sounds, meant to convey solace. I'm the one who goes to funerals, who delivers eulogies, who always remembers to write to the bereaved. Then I tell him that if I only have to have radiation, I will simply get my hair cut a couple of inches, as I do every few months anyway. But if I have to undergo chemotherapy, too, I will have my hair cut very short, like a boy's, which is something I kind of want to try anyway but am afraid to, as it might look bad and would take a long time to grow out. I have already e-mailed Binky in New York, explaining that if I'm going to lose all my hair, I want an authentic Yankees baseball cap to wear, and not one of the cheap knock-offs that they make in Britain.

"Fine," he says. But it's not fine, it's not fine at all.

"I'm not supposed to be here," I repeat.

"So get up and take a walk," my husband says. Together, we do laps around the tenth-floor ward.

On my second-to-last day in the hospital, Rabbi Stan gets through to me, phoning through to the nurse's station, and I tell him that somewhere—perhaps in one of those alternative-medicine books by Andrew Weil that I started reading after my mother got sick—I'd read that cancer was a gift. Or maybe not. Maybe I've made that one up. "Have you heard of this?" I ask him. "Can't say that I have," he says. He is awkward on the phone—his long-distance bedside manner a little stiff. "The idea," I tell him, "is that cancer lets you let go of all your baggage. That is, if it doesn't kill you first."

"When do you go home?" he says.

"Tomorrow."

"Baruch ha Shem."

But, perversely, I don't really want to go home—home to our small rented house, with its dark colors, narrow rooms, and views of the Kelvin River. I like it here in the hospital, here with the other women, chatting. I like the nurses, the doctors, the residents. I like the good cleaning lady who brings us bits of hospital gossip and the bad cleaning lady who barely moves the dirt around but calls us "love" and "hen." I like being served tea in bed, and the smell of the flowers that are filling up the room, and the sense of being in a spaceship, cozened and protected from the world. Most of all I like the routine that allows me to blot out thoughts of Friday. What I'll learn on Friday. What my doctors will tell me about what they find under the microscope on Friday. And then: Shabbat!

But I have to go home, home to our little, cozy, furnished house, our Glasgow nest. My drains are clear. My family needs me.

I am always worried about running out of material, about my well running dry, even though my Baton Rouge psychotherapist has told me time and time again that the well will always be there, that it will not run dry, that it is my soul. Now I know that this is true. When my brother-in-law David calls from his home in Jerusalem, he says: "So I guess you've got all kinds of new things to write about." He is an editor at the *Jerusalem Report*, an English-language bimonthly, and understands something of inspiration, deadlines, the way ideas can enter your mind, like birds, squawking, and just as quickly fly off. "Are you taking notes?" he asks.

Yes, I tell him. *Yes I am.*

13

Signs

I have to admit that spending six months in chemotherapy and radiation wasn't on the top of my to-do list for our year abroad, but if I could rewrite my own personal history, go back and do it all over again, I wouldn't edit out any of it: not the fear, not the hair loss, not the nausea, not the tears. Cancer was the best thing that ever happened to me, because it taught me something that I had never really known before, and that is, simply, that I am loved. And when I was finished, and my hair began to grow back again, I knew that I hadn't been spared in order to set the world on fire or because I'm some kind of saint, but, rather, merely so that I might walk the path I was intended to walk. That I might claim my gifts. That I might, in my own way, sing.

God has not yet spoken to me, and I somehow doubt that He ever will—at least not in the way that He speaks to Joanna—in a way I can hear, as I hear my children when, in the middle of the night, they appear at my bedside with a bad dream. On the other hand, I like to think that I heard the voice of God when I heard the women singing at St. Anthony's, or again, in the middle of the drugged night, when I heard the workmen singing outside my hospital room in Glasgow. I like to think that God sent Gerald to me not as a distillation of the Gerald who once walked the earth but as a symbol of divine love, coming to me in a shape I could understand. So, too, I think God appears in every act of kindness, and in Glasgow, in the wake of my illness, kindness poured down on me like warm spring showers. My friend Debra signed on to accompany me to all eight of my chemotherapy sessions. My hospital roommates and I regularly got together for lunch, and over the course of my treatment I called on each of them for solace and strength. I soon began hearing from both sides of the Atlantic that Catholics were lighting candles for me, Baptists were stomping and dancing, Jews were praying for a *refuah shlemah* (a complete healing), and in upstate New York my friend Alice's Buddhist mother's monk was chanting. My husband told people: "Jennifer's not taking any chances." But as far as I was concerned, I was merely asking for help. In Baton Rouge, God regularly makes personal appearances to the faithful and even shows up on billboards along I-10, where He proclaims His Word and then signs off with His Name. My favorite billboard is the one that hovers along a particularly ugly stretch of the interstate between the old riverfront downtown and the petrochemical plants that cluster north of the airport. "Looking for a sign from God?" it says. "Here it is!"

Looking for a sign from God? How about the time I was riding to the airport in a taxicab, shaking with my usual pre-airplane anxiety attack, and noticed, on the floor beside my feet, a book called *The God Search*? What the hell. No one was around. I opened it and inside I read that God was always with you, even when you were certain that He was far away. Was that a sign? Why not? How about the fact that after an almost thirty-year hiatus, I started painting again, painting as I had as a child, my hands vibrating with the desire to hold a paintbrush? How about dreaming in Hebrew? Seeing lightning streak across the sky? Hearing words form in my head and then looking up to realize that I had written an entire short story in the voice of someone I'd never met before? And what am I to make of the lovely if somewhat dotty elderly lady at Beth Shalom who, every time she sees me, clasps my hands in hers and says, "You are a blessing." Holding my sister Binky's two baby girls? What about the fact that my mother, despite everything, was still alive when we returned to America, still alive when Sam at last ascended the bimah and became a bar mitzvah? She flew down to Baton Rouge with my father and sat front and center in a wheelchair, my father by her side.

What am I to make of the fact that I was with my grandmother, the Nana whom I adored, when she finally died? She died two months after her ninety-sixth birthday, in the home in Washington that my parents had moved her into years earlier. I just happened to be in town that weekend, visiting my mother. I sat by Nana's bed in the small room that had become her entire world and talked about Daddy Lee and Henderson Grandma, Mommy Les and Cousin Babette, and when she shuddered and died, I finally knew why it was that I had been entrusted with her stories.

In a poem that has been incorporated into the Reform Jewish prayer book, the late Rabbi Alvin Fine wrote:

> Birth is a beginning
> And death a destination
> But life is a journey
> A going—a growing
> From stage to stage
> From childhood to maturity
> And youth to age.
> From innocence to awareness
> And ignorance to knowing;
> From foolishness to discretion
> And then perhaps, to wisdom.
> From weakness to strength
> Or strength to weakness
> And, often, back again.
> From health to sickness
> And back we pray, to health again.
> From offense to forgiveness,
> From loneliness to love,
> From joy to gratitude,
> From pain to compassion,
> And grief to understanding—
> From fear to faith.
> From defeat to defeat to defeat—
> Until, looking backward or ahead,
> We see that victory lies
> Not as some high place along the way,
> But in having made the journey, stage by stage.
> A sacred pilgrimage.
> Birth is a beginning
> And death a destination.
> But life is a journey,
> A sacred pilgrimage.

Which brings me, at last, to my mother. Two months after Nana took her last breath, my father called me in Baton Rouge to tell me to get on the next plane, explaining that Mom had collapsed and was now lying in bed, barely conscious. A few hours later, on the telephone, I told my mother that I was on my way. "Can't wait!" she said. But she did wait. In fact, she waited until after four o'clock in the afternoon of the next day to quietly die the death she'd prayed for, at home, without pain, and surrounded by her family, my father—the only man she had ever loved—never leaving her side.

My mother! As I write this, I can feel her hands on my shoulders and hear her voice whispering in my ear: "Just tell the truth, Jennifer. Just tell the truth."

The truth is, I don't know what the truth is. I only know what's in my own imperfect heart.

Postscript
After the Storm

When Katrina, and then Rita, roared ashore, altering both the landscape and the American psyche, I found myself doing something I never would have been able to do had Stuart not dragged me and the kids down to Baton Rouge, where I found myself, both at St. Anthony's and at Beth Shalom, surrounded by people whose deepest desire was to walk with God. In a shelter that had been set up in an abandoned K-Mart on Airline Highway, I worked—along with hundreds of medical and nonmedical volunteers from all over the country—tending to the sick and the desperate, giving sponge-baths, dispensing stuffed animals, and helping people who could barely walk get to the toilet or finding them something to eat. People I'd never before met and would no doubt never see again sobbed in my arms. Old men clutched my hand; Vietnam vets begged me to help them find relatives lost in the storm; people who'd spent days waist-high in filthy water or praying for their lives inside the New Orleans Superdome or the Civic Center blessed me, saying that I was an angel, and that God was good, and that the shelter itself—with its ancient grime, buzzing, fluorescent lighting, and almost complete lack of plumbing—was heaven.

In the fifth-century book the *Pesikta de-Rav Kahana* it is written: "Between the Garden of Eden and Gehenna (hell) there is no more than the breadth of a hand."

Dear God, my heavenly Father, Source of All Life, guide my hands.